It's another Quality Book from CGP

This book is for anyone studying _Twelfth Night_ at GCSE.

Studying Shakespeare can give you a real headache,
but happily this CGP book makes your life just a little bit easier.
We've crammed in absolutely everything you'll need to write about
— and there are tips on essay skills to top it all off.

It's also got some daft bits in to try and make the whole
experience at least vaguely entertaining for you.

What CGP is all about

Our sole aim here at CGP is to produce the highest quality books
— carefully written, immaculately presented and dangerously
close to being funny.

Then we work our socks off to get them out to you
— at the cheapest possible prices.

CONTENTS

Published by Coordination Group Publications, Ltd.

Contributors:
Taissa Csáky
Tim Major
Becky May
Katherine Reed
William Shakespeare

ISBN: 1-84146-117-2
Groovy website: www.cgpbooks.co.uk
Jolly bits of clipart from CorelDRAW
Printed by Elanders Hindson, Newcastle upon Tyne.
Text, design, layout and original illustrations © Coordination Group Publications Ltd. 2002

What You Have to Do

The point is to get <u>good marks</u> in your <u>essays</u>. This page does exactly what it says on the tin.

Include *These Three Things in Your Essay*

1) **KNOWLEDGE** ➤ You should know the <u>events</u> and <u>characters</u> in the play in detail — so you can <u>describe</u> them accurately, and <u>discuss</u> them confidently, in your essay.

2) **UNDERSTANDING** ➤ <u>Knowing facts</u> about the play <u>isn't enough</u>.
By the time you write your essay you should:

> • Understand the main <u>themes</u> and <u>ideas</u> in the play.
> • Understand the <u>structure</u> and <u>stagecraft</u> of the play.
> • Know a bit about the <u>historical context</u> of the play.

3) **OPINION**

• People can <u>interpret</u> the play in <u>different</u> ways. To get good marks you need to include your <u>opinion</u> about the <u>play</u> and the essay <u>topic</u>. <u>Explain</u> your opinion <u>clearly</u> and back it up with <u>examples</u> from the text.

• To get the higher marks, discuss the <u>different opinions</u> people could have about the essay topic. Argue <u>why</u> the opinion you agree with is <u>better</u> than the others. Again, it's really important to <u>support</u> your <u>argument</u> with <u>examples</u>.

You'll Have to Answer *Essay Questions* Like These

1) Do you find Malvolio sympathetic or repulsive? How do your feelings about his character change throughout the play?

> *For this type of question read up on **Characters**.*

2) How do the characters of Sir Toby and Sir Andrew add to the humour of the play? You might wish to consider:
   • their language
   • the trick on Malvolio
   • the contrast between them and other characters

> *For this type of question look at **Language** and **Stagecraft**.*

3) In Act 4 Scene 1, Feste says:
   "Nothing that is so, is so."
   To what extent is the plot of Twelfth Night based on misunderstandings? Describe three examples from the play, and discuss the consequences of each misunderstanding.

> *Use **What Happens in the Play** to pick the events.*

4) Compare and contrast Viola's love for Orsino with Orsino's love for Olivia. Whose love is stronger?

> *For this type of question read up on **Themes** and **Characters**.*

Tripping the Twelfth Night fantastic...

Don't get scared by this page. By the end of the book all this stuff will be at your toe-tips.
Order in the pizza and get learning. Life is good...

Why the Play Seems Weird

Lots of the things that seem weird in *Twelfth Night* weren't weird when it was written.
You've got to know what they are — it's the only way to answer essay questions properly.

Don't Forget the Play is Around 400 Years Old

Phew — that's pretty old for anything, especially a play. It's like an episode of Eastenders still being popular in the year 2400. It's not surprising that a lot of it seems strange nowadays.

The play's set in Illyria — a far-off, exotic place.
That's why everyone's got funny-sounding names.

People Must've had a Weird Sense of Humour then

A lot's changed since Shakespeare wrote *Twelfth Night* — including people's sense of humour.

1) One thing people used to find particularly rib-tickling was the idea of women dressing up as men. The main character, Viola, pretends to be a boy called Cesario for most of the play.

2) It's funny because everybody else thinks she really is a boy, and they make all sorts of embarrassing mistakes.

3) The play's full of other stupid misunderstandings too. Maria and Sir Toby play a trick on Malvolio, and there's even a jester who goes around cracking silly jokes.

4) Most of the jokes are puns — words with double meanings. People thought they were hilarious in Shakespeare's time.

It's Meant to be Acted — Not Just Read

1) *Twelfth Night* is a play, not a book — it's meant to be seen on a stage with actors playing the parts.

2) When you read it, all you get is what the characters say. It's often pretty hard to follow what's going on.

3) It makes more sense if you imagine what's happening. Think about what the characters are like, and how you think they would speak and act.

4) If you can, watch a film version of the play. It's a great way to bring it to life.

Dressing up as men — it's a bit of a drag...

OK, Shakespeare's a bit strange, but hey, get over it. It was written ages ago, so not only was the language different, the humour was really different as well. (Apart from the puns, which are always hilarious, of course.)

Tricky Play Stuff

If there were <u>no misunderstandings</u> and <u>nothing silly</u> ever happened, it'd be a pretty <u>dull play</u>. You have to remember that Shakespeare's <u>not trying</u> to be <u>realistic</u>, just to <u>entertain people</u>.

It's Meant to be Watched by an Audience

The whole point of a play is it <u>tells a story</u> by <u>showing you</u> what happened. You don't just hear the words — you see people talking and fighting. Anybody <u>watching</u> the play is part of the <u>audience</u>.

I'm not doing this, if he's not even going to watch.

The Idea is to Make the Audience Laugh

1) The things that <u>happen</u> and the things people <u>say</u> in the play are there to make the audience feel different <u>moods</u>. Because <u>Twelfth Night</u>'s a comedy, <u>most</u> of the things that happen are meant to make the audience <u>laugh</u>.

2) The play <u>isn't just</u> funny. There are <u>other</u> moods the audience could feel too. They could <u>feel sorry</u> for Malvolio at the end of the play.

3) You'll get <u>loads of marks</u> for your essays if you say what the <u>audience feels</u> about a scene. That just means saying what <u>you feel</u> when you <u>read</u> it. Don't forget to give <u>examples</u> from the scene to <u>back up</u> what you're saying.

Don't Confuse Characters with Actors

It's simple enough — <u>characters</u> are the people in the story, like Viola, Olivia and Orsino. The <u>actors</u> are the people who play them. <u>Don't</u> get them confused.

Malvolio is a <u>character</u>. Richard Briers is an <u>actor</u> who played Malvolio.

Sometimes Characters Talk to Themselves

One of the really odd things about <u>Twelfth Night</u> is when characters <u>talk to themselves</u>. Don't worry — they haven't suddenly gone barmy.

These bits are called <u>soliloquies</u>.

<u>Viola</u> does it at the end of Act 2, Scene 2. <u>Malvolio</u> does it in Act 2, Scene 5, reading the letter aloud and saying what he thinks about it. In Act 4, Scene 3 <u>Sebastian</u> talks to himself about marrying Olivia.

It's a way for the audience to find out what a character's <u>thinking</u> — the character just says it <u>out loud</u>.

Make the audience laugh? — he'd need nitrous oxide...

It stands to reason — if you go to see a play, you want to be <u>entertained</u>. Shakespeare's plays would have been a <u>big flop</u> if the audience didn't have a good time. So that meant adding <u>humour</u>, <u>pathos</u>, <u>gore</u>... and getting <u>good actors</u> to play the parts. Just like <u>Hollywood</u> really... ish.

Tricky Play Words

Hey kids — <u>jargon time</u>. ☺ This page trawls through all those <u>fancy play words</u> that keep coming up. You need to <u>know what they mean</u> so get on with it.

Twelfth Night *is a* Comedy

A <u>comedy</u> is meant to make the audience <u>laugh</u>.

Although things may go wrong in a comedy story, <u>nothing</u> goes <u>seriously</u> wrong.

There's always a <u>happy ending</u>. In Shakespeare's comedies it's usually a <u>wedding</u>.

It's Divided into Acts *and* Scenes

1) The play is divided into <u>five</u> big sections, called <u>acts</u>. Each act is like an <u>episode</u> of a TV serial — lots of things happen in it, but it's only <u>part</u> of the whole thing.

2) Each act is made up of <u>smaller</u> sections called <u>scenes</u>. There's nothing complicated about them. A scene shows you a <u>small bit</u> of the story and then ends. Then a <u>new scene</u> starts that shows you the <u>next bit</u>.

3) Scenes are just a way of <u>breaking up</u> the story. They show that time has passed in the story — <u>one scene</u> could be set in the <u>evening</u> and the <u>next one</u> on the <u>following day</u>.

4) They also let the play <u>move</u> to <u>different places</u> — one scene will happen at Olivia's house, the next one at Duke Orsino's etc.

Stage Directions *Say What the Characters are* Doing

Stage directions are little phrases that describe the characters' actions.

e.g.   *Clock strikes*   *Draws his dagger*

These are the really common ones in the play:

Enter = when someone comes <u>onto</u> the stage

Exit = when <u>one</u> person <u>leaves</u> the stage

Exeunt = when <u>more than one</u> person leaves the stage

Aside = to show a character's talking to <u>himself</u> or <u>herself</u>

That act — it was the worst I've ever scene...

You've got to <u>get used</u> to these <u>technical play words</u> — they come up again and again.

How the Play Was Acted

In the early 1600s people just wanted to have a <u>good time</u> at the theatre, and the fact that there was <u>no scenery</u> or <u>actresses</u> wasn't going to stop them.

All the Actors Were Men

1) In Shakespeare's day, <u>women</u> were expected to behave <u>respectably</u> — which meant they <u>weren't</u> allowed to act in the theatre.

2) That meant that any <u>female</u> characters were played by <u>men</u> — which could have been a bit confusing.

3) Female characters were normally played by <u>young boys</u> because they were <u>less masculine</u> and had <u>higher voices</u>.

4) The character of Viola in *Twelfth Night* is a bit of a joke, because it would have been a <u>man</u> playing a <u>woman</u> pretending to be a <u>man</u>.

There Was No Scenery

1) When *Twelfth Night* was first performed they <u>didn't bother</u> with backdrops or fancy sets. Only things that were <u>important</u> to the plot were on stage (like the hedge that Fabian, Sir Andrew and Sir Toby hide behind).

2) Instead, Shakespeare had to tell people <u>where</u> each scene was set by mentioning it in the <u>dialogue</u>.

3) The plays were always performed in the <u>afternoon</u>, so characters also had to <u>explain</u> if a scene was supposed to be happening at <u>night</u>.

Theatres Were Rowdy and Fun

Even though Shakespeare's plays can seem a bit stuffy nowadays, people used to think they were a great excuse for a <u>rowdy day out</u>.

1) Going to the theatre <u>wasn't</u> very <u>comfortable</u>. Lots of the people at Shakespeare's <u>Globe</u> theatre in London had to <u>stand</u> the whole way through the play, and wouldn't have been able to sit quietly and watch it even if they'd wanted to.

2) There were loads of <u>hecklers</u>. People <u>didn't</u> take plays too <u>seriously</u> and would have <u>talked</u> through the play — and they sometimes <u>shouted</u> at the actors.

3) There might have been some <u>audience participation</u>, like in a pantomime. People might have <u>hissed</u> when Malvolio came on stage, or <u>cheered</u> when Orsino says he'll marry Viola.

Get him off! What a load of rubbish!

Try going to your local theatre and badgering the actors — then claiming that's what Shakespeare would have wanted. Go on, it'll be a laugh. Hilarious, in fact. (Just don't mention my name, OK...)

Why the Play's in Poetry and Prose

This is a mega-important bit. You need to learn why some parts of the play are in poetry and the others are in prose. It'll really help you understand what's going on in each scene.

Shakespeare Uses Poetry for Formal or Serious Bits

All the serious bits in *Twelfth Night* tend to be in poetry.

1) Every time Orsino speaks, he uses poetry. It shows he's dead posh and a noble.

> I know thy constellation is right apt
> For this affair. Some four or five attend him;
> *Act 1, Scene 4, 34-35*

2) Viola/Cesario always speaks to Orsino in poetry — their conversations are always really formal.

> VIOLA   Sir, shall I to this lady?
> ORSINO   Ay, that's the theme.
> *Act 2, Scene 4, 119*

3) All the serious bits about love are in poetry — like all the bits between Olivia and Viola/Cesario, and Olivia and Sebastian.

> OLIVIA   Nay, come, I prithee. Would thoud'st be ruled by me!
> SEBASTIAN Madam, I will.
> OLIVIA   O, say so, and so be!
> *Act 4, Scene 1, 58-59*

He Uses Prose for the Comedy Bits

Everything's a crazy mess in these scenes — nobody's following the rules.
That's why the characters speak prose in the comedy scenes.
They aren't following the rules for poetry.

1) All the comic characters, like Sir Andrew, Sir Toby and Feste always speak in prose.

2) The scenes about the trick on Malvolio are all in prose.

3) Viola and Sebastian use prose with Malvolio, Feste, Toby and Andrew.

> Anyone in the play who isn't posh speaks prose.

In Some Scenes He uses a Mixture of Both

In Act 1, Scene 5, Viola/Cesario starts off speaking to Olivia in prose, but changes to poetry. Olivia starts in prose too, but also changes to poetry.

The end of the play is in poetry except for a few speeches. Everything's being sorted out and put back into order — Feste, Sir Toby and Sir Andrew still speak prose; everyone else speaks poetry.

"Thy constellation is right apt" for this exam...*

Don't forget — scenes with poetry are formal or serious, scenes with prose are usually comedy bits.

How to Read the Poetry

It's a pain in the neck, but you've got to know how to read the poetry in the play.

The Poetry Always Has Ten or Eleven Syllables

Every line of poetry in the play has got ten or eleven syllables — or beats.

1 2 3 4 5 6 7 8 9 10
If music be the food of love, play on,

This is what makes the poetry tricky to read — Shakespeare fiddles with the words to make them fit into lines of ten or eleven syllables with this rhythm.

① He changes the order of the words to make them fit the line.

> A most extracting frenzy of mine own
> From my remembrance clearly banished his.
> *Act 5, Scene 1, 270-271*

= a most extracting frenzy of mine clearly banished his (frenzy) from my remembrance.

② Sometimes he makes a word last for an extra syllable.

Normally "fixed" has one syllable — but here you have to say it "fix - ed" so that there are ten syllables in the line.

> And tell them, there thy fixèd foot shall grow
> Till thou have audience.
> *Act 1, Scene 4, 17-18*

③ Worst of all, he even leaves whole words out — which is a pain.

> He left this ring behind him,
> Would I, or not. Tell him, I'll none of it.
> *Act 1, Scene 5, 277-278*

"Tell him I'll none of it" doesn't seem to make any sense — Shakespeare's left out the word "have" so the line only has ten syllables.

Don't Stop Reading at the End of Each Line

1) Even though each line starts with a capital letter, it doesn't mean it's a separate sentence. Just ignore the capitals and follow the punctuation.

> I hate ingratitude more in a man
> Than lying, vainness, babbling and drunkenness,
> Or any taint of vice whose strong corruption
> Inhabits our frail blood.   *Act 3, Scene 4, 323-326*

There's no full stop so carry on to the next line.

2) There isn't a break in the sentence even when it moves to the next line. You've got to read it as if it's written like this:

> I hate ingratitude more in a man than lying, vainness, babbling and drunkenness, or any taint of vice whose strong corruption inhabits our frail blood.

If poetry be the food of love I'll eat my hat...

Every line of poetry in the play has ten or eleven syllables — learn that and the rest'll start to follow.

Different Kinds of Poetry

Not all poems lead to Rome... or something. Shakespeare uses <u>different kinds</u> of poetry for <u>different moods</u>. Read on — it's a <u>laugh a minute</u>...

Most of the Play's in Blank Verse — It Doesn't Rhyme

It's a stupid name, blank verse — all it really means is any bits of poetry that <u>don't rhyme</u>. One key thing that shows they're poetry is the number of <u>syllables</u> in each line — yep, you've guessed it, <u>ten</u> or <u>eleven</u>.

Here's a line of blank verse.

> O then, unfold the passion of my love,
> Act 1, Scene 4, 23

This gets really hairy when <u>two people</u> are talking. Their <u>conversation</u> has to <u>fit</u> into lines of poetry.

This is still <u>poetry</u>, remember.

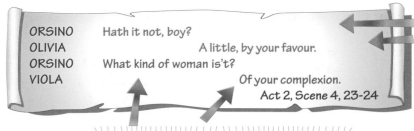

ORSINO	Hath it not, boy?
OLIVIA	A little, by your favour.
ORSINO	What kind of woman is't?
VIOLA	Of your complexion.
	Act 2, Scene 4, 23-24

These two bits form <u>one line</u> — that's why they're written like this.

<u>These two bits</u> together make <u>another</u> line.

Some Bits of it Rhyme

Some parts of the play have <u>bits</u> of rhyme in them — especially at the <u>end</u> of scenes. If most of a scene <u>doesn't</u> rhyme but a tiny bit of it <u>does</u>, mention it in your answer.

> Fate, show thy force; ourselves we do not owe.
> What is decreed must be — and be this so.
> Act 1, Scene 5, 286-287

Little <u>tricks</u> like this <u>help</u> your answer no end.

Feste Sings Lots of Songs too

Feste's songs are really important for setting the <u>mood</u> of scenes — that means they're well worth <u>writing about</u>. He sings several <u>sad love songs</u>, and one at the <u>end</u> of the play.

And now the end is near; and so I face the final curtain...

It's all about how <u>life changes</u> as you get <u>older</u>. The last verse <u>finishes</u> off the whole play.

> A great while ago the world begun,
> With hey, ho, the wind and the rain,
> But that's all one, our play is done,
> And we'll strive to please you every day.
> Act 5, Scene 1, 389-392

Shakespeare's verse — blank and you'll miss it...

It <u>isn't</u> just about Shakespeare writing poetry — it's about the <u>kinds of poetry</u> he uses in different scenes. You need to be able to <u>recognise</u> each kind so you can <u>write</u> about them in your essay.

How to Read the Prose

Prose is anything that <u>isn't</u> written in poetry — it <u>doesn't</u> have to have any rhymes or rhythm. That's the <u>good news</u>. The <u>bad news</u> is it's <u>just as tricky</u> to read. Humph.

The <u>Big Problem</u> — <u>Prose has Lots of</u> <u>Long Sentences</u>

Here's the <u>tricky</u> part — all those blinking <u>long sentences</u>. You've got to read them <u>really carefully</u> to make sure you <u>understand</u> what they mean.

> He will come to her in yellow stockings, and 'tis a colour she abhors, and cross-gartered, a fashion she detests — and he will smile upon her, which will now be so unsuitable to her disposition, being addicted to a melancholy as she is, that it cannot but turn him into a notable contempt.
>
> Act 2, Scene 5, 176-181

Phew — see what I mean. You'll need to <u>read</u> sentences like this a <u>few times</u> to make sense of them. The secret is to <u>break it up</u> into smaller bits.

He will come to her in yellow stockings,   and 'tis a colour she abhors,

and cross-gartered,   a fashion she detests;

These are the <u>first four bits</u> of the sentence. It's much easier to <u>work out</u> what they <u>mean</u> now.

Malvolio will go to Olivia in yellow stockings and cross-gartered. She hates yellow and she hates cross-gartering.

All the <u>Letters</u> <u>in the Play are in</u> <u>Prose</u>

You need to <u>watch out</u> for <u>letters</u> in the play — there are several <u>important</u> ones.

(1) Malvolio finds a <u>fake letter</u> — he <u>thinks</u> it's from Olivia but <u>Maria</u> actually wrote it.

> In my stars I am above thee, but be not afraid of greatness. Some are born great, some achieve greatness, and some have greatness thrust upon 'em.
>
> Act 2, Scene 5, 125-128

It's written in <u>fancy language</u> to sound <u>posh</u> and <u>grand</u> so that Malvolio <u>believes</u> it's from Olivia.

(2) Sir Andrew's challenge to Viola/Cesario is <u>supposed</u> to sound <u>grand</u> and <u>threatening</u>, but it ends up sounding <u>silly</u> instead.

> 'Fare thee well, and God have mercy upon one of our souls! He may have mercy upon mine, but my hope is better, and so look to thyself.'
>
> Act 3, Scene 4, 149-151

Jolly good luck, old thing. Oh no, you're fighting me, aren't you? Well, in that case, hope you lose, monkey-boy.

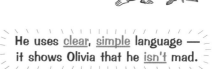

(3) In the <u>last scene</u> of the play, <u>Malvolio</u> sends a letter to Olivia asking <u>why</u> he's been so badly treated.

> Though you have put me into darkness, and given your drunken cousin rule over me, yet have I the benefit of my senses as well as your ladyship.
>
> Act 5, Scene 1, 289-291

He uses <u>clear</u>, <u>simple</u> language — it shows Olivia that he <u>isn't</u> mad.

Old Words and Fancy Words

<u>Old-fashioned language</u> — you know the score, loads of <u>thees and thous</u> all over the place...
<u>You need to know</u>: a) what they all <u>mean</u> — and b) <u>who</u> uses them and <u>when</u>.

Here are Some Common Old Words

These <u>words</u> turn up all the time — they make sentences <u>look</u> much <u>harder</u> than they really are.

1)   Thou = You   Thee = You   Thy = Your

The characters use "<u>thou</u>", "<u>thee</u>" and "<u>thy</u>" when
they're talking to <u>friends</u> or people they <u>know well</u>:

> Fare thee well.
> Act 3, Scene 4, 198

Olivia is speaking
affectionately to
Cesario/Viola.

They also use them when they're talking
to people of a <u>lower social class</u>.

Orsino calls Cesario/Viola "thou", but <u>she</u> always calls <u>him</u> "you".

> What dost thou know?
> Act 2, Scene 4, 101

> But if she cannot love you, sir?
> Act 2, Scene 4, 84

Characters also use them when they're <u>insulting</u> someone.

> If thou thou'st him some thrice, it shall not be amiss —
> Act 3, Scene 2, 39-40

Sir Toby is saying that Sir Andrew should call
Cesario "thou" lots in his challenge as an <u>insult</u>.

2)   Art = are   wilt = will   hast = has

Verbs like these go with "thou"

> How now, art thou mad?.
> Act 5, Scene 1, 281

3)   Hither = to here

> He shall enlarge him — fetch Malvolio hither.
> Act 5, Scene 1, 267

4)   Prithee = I pray thee/I ask you

> Prithee, be content —
> Act 5, Scene 1, 336

5)   Hath = has

> He hath not told us of the captain yet.
> Act 5, Scene 1, 365

Watch Out for Fancy Words as well

Shakespeare never uses two words when he can use ten. It can get seriously <u>confusing</u>
when he uses loads of <u>fancy-sounding</u> words that really mean something <u>simple</u> and <u>easy</u>.

> He finishèd indeed his mortal act
> That day that made my sister thirteen years.
> Act 5, Scene 1, 236-7

This looks nasty and hard —
but here's what it <u>really means</u>.

He died on my sister's thirteenth birthday.

All those thous are enough to make you wilt...

The <u>lingo</u> can get a bit funny sometimes — <u>learning</u> these <u>dusty old words</u> will really help you out.

Revision Summary

Shakespeare uses a lot of old and fancy words... And don't forget all that poetry either. Make sure you've been through this section carefully — it'll help you to spot the different tricks Shakespeare uses in some scenes. So, on to these revision questions. I know they're a pain, but they're the only way you can test what you know. If you get stuck go back and look over the section again. Then have another go. You should be getting the whole lot absolutely right before you move on.

1) Complete this sentence: Plays are meant to be...
   a) ...read in silence   b) ...acted on stage   c) ...flushed down the toilet.

2) What is an audience?

3) What's the difference between characters and actors?

4) Why do people talk to themselves in the play?

5) What is an Act?

6) What is a Scene?

7) What are the stage directions?

8) Complete the sentence: In Shakespeare's time, all of the actors were...
   a) ...men   b) ...women   c) ...children   d) ...absolutely pants.

9) How did Shakespeare let the audience know where a scene was set?

10) Give three reasons why the theatre would have been a rowdy place to be in the early 1600s.

11) When does Shakespeare use poetry in the play?

12) When does he use prose?

13) How many syllables does every line of poetry have?

14) What three things does Shakespeare sometimes do to make words fit the line?

15) Why shouldn't you stop reading at the end of each line of poetry?

16) What is blank verse?

17) What do Feste's songs help to do?

18) What is prose?

19) What makes Shakespeare's prose difficult to read?

20) Are the letters in the play written in poetry or prose?

21) What do "thou" and "thee" mean? What does "thy" mean?

22) What does "prithee" mean?

Where the Play's Set

Shakespeare wanted lots of ridiculous things to happen in *Twelfth Night* so he set it in Illyria — a long way from England. It helped make the story more believable for his audience.

Illyria *is Partly* Real *and Partly* Imaginary

1) Illyria is the area on the Mediterranean where Slovenia, Croatia, Bosnia, and Serbia are today.

2) At the time Shakespeare was writing the play those places belonged to Venice. A hundred years before, Venice had been one of the richest cities in the world, and it still sounded like a glamorous place.

3) The name Illyria would have made the audience think of a warm, wealthy and beautiful country.

4) The real Illyria was probably quite different from the one in the play. Shakespeare wasn't trying to be realistic — he was trying to describe a place where the audience can believe strange things could happen.

> Shakespeare probably **never** went to the real Illyria.
> He got his ideas about what it might be like from books.

It's a Very Different Society — With Stricter Rules

When Shakespeare wrote *Twelfth Night* Queen Elizabeth 1 ruled England. Powerful nobles helped her to rule. Nobles were expected to look after the country and the people in it. In return everyone else was expected to give the nobles obedience and respect.

1) Orsino is the Duke of Illyria. He rules the country like a king. Olivia is a Countess. That makes her a noble too. They are from the most important and powerful level of society.

2) Olivia and Orsino's households are like mini-kingdoms, and Olivia and Orsino are the rulers of their families and servants. Everyone in the household needs to treat them with respect if they want to stay.

3) You were also supposed to respect other people:

> Malvolio is the Steward in Olivia's house. The Steward organises the house so Olivia doesn't have to — he's like a manager.

> Viola/Cesario has joined Orsino's household as a courtier. That means she's not a servant, and the servants like Malvolio and Fabian should look up to her.

4) The original audience would have been quite shocked at seeing characters behave the way they do in the play. They thought it was dangerous — if people broke the rules, then society could fall apart.

He knew nothing about Illyria — he was talking out of his

Shakespeare's quite cunning here. (Yeah, OK, just hear me out.) He uses a different setting so that his characters can do whatever he wants them to without it being too scandalous. It means he can get away with murder. Well, cross-dressing, disobedience, lack of respect for noblemen...

Midwinter Madness

In *Twelfth Night* many of the characters act as if they're temporarily mad. To excuse their odd behaviour, Shakespeare called the play after a festival when everybody behaved in a crazy way.

The Social Rules Get Broken in Twelfth Night

In *Twelfth Night* Shakespeare takes away the normal rules about how people should behave. People act out of character, and do things which don't suit their social position.

1) Taking away the rules like Shakespeare does in *Twelfth Night* is what used to happen at the Feast of Fools. This was a huge midwinter party held every year on 6th January. Another name for 6th January is Twelfth Night, because it is twelve days after Christmas Day.

Tom and Sir Prance-a-lot pick up ideas for their Feast of Fools costumes.

2) At the Feast of Fools servants would dress up as lords and ladies, and the nobles could behave in a more silly and undignified way than usual. A 'Lord of Misrule' was chosen to play tricks on the guests.

3) The events in the play don't happen on Twelfth Night, but nearly all the characters behave as though they were at a Feast of Fools party. Everything's all gone crazy.

Love Makes the Characters Act Strangely

Most of the weirdness comes from people falling in love. It makes them do daft things. In those days, people thought love was a kind of madness.

Olivia's love for Cesario makes her lose track of what's going on in her household. In the last scene she even says that she was a bit mad:

> A most extracting frenzy of mine own
> From my remembrance clearly banished his.
> Act 5, Scene 1, 270-271

Orsino says he's in love with Olivia — for most of the play he mopes around listening to miserable music and moaning about his love like a big jessie.

Malvolio and Antonio also do stupid things out of love — Malvolio tries to impress Olivia, and Antonio follows Sebastian to Illyria even though his life's in danger.

No One's Really Mad — They just Seem Mad

Other characters seem mad because it's the easiest way to explain their odd behaviour.

When Malvolio starts acting weirdly, Olivia thinks he's mad. She lets Sir Toby lock him up as a madman.

> Why, this is very midsummer madness.
> Act 3, Scene 4, 52

Sebastian wonders if Sir Andrew and Sir Toby are mad when they attack him thinking he's Cesario:

> Are all the people mad?
> Act 4, Scene 1, 23

Wahey, it's Twelfth Night — let's go crazy... uh... yeah...

Ah, love makes fools out of everyone... In plays anyway. While the rest of us just get a bit embarrassed, they go wearing yellow stockings and getting off with people's twin brothers...

Love

Love is one of the main themes of the play. Ick.

People Imagined Love Differently in the 1600s

Ideas about love and marriage were very different in Elizabethan England than they are now:

1) Arranged marriages were normal. It was also OK to marry someone for their money and land.

2) Society was very male-dominated — women were thought of as mentally weaker than men, and wives were often thought of as possessions.

3) Ideals in literature and plays about what love should be like were also different. Stories of Courtly Love told of men suffering hardships to gain the love of 'perfect', almost unattainable women. Orsino thinks of himself as a character in one of those stories.

The Play Shows Many Kinds of Love

FRIENDSHIP Antonio feels brotherly love for Sebastian.

> If you will not murder me for my love, let me be your servant.
> Antonio, Act 2, Scene 1, 30-31

TRUE LOVE Viola is constant in her love for Orsino.

> After him I love,
> More than I love these eyes, more than my life
> Viola, Act 5, Scene 1, 127-128

RESPECT Sir Toby likes Maria's mischievous nature.

> She's a beagle, true-bred, and one that adores me
> Sir Toby, Act 2, Scene 3, 165

COURTLY LOVE Orsino fancies himself as a hero in a romantic novel.

> For such as I am, all true lovers are
> Orsino, Act 2, Scene 4, 15

INFATUATION Olivia is smitten with Cesario's looks.

> Even so quickly may one catch the plague?
> Olivia on fancying Cesario, Act 1, Scene 5, 271

Shakespeare's Attitude to Love is Quite Modern

Twelfth Night twists standard 17th-century attitudes about love into something a bit different.

Orsino likes to think of himself suffering for the love of a beautiful woman. At the end it turns out his feelings for Olivia weren't very deep.

> Get thee to yond same sovereign cruelty.
> Tell her my love, more noble than the world,
> Orsino, Act 2, Scene 4, 77-78

> There is no woman's sides
> Can bide the beating of so strong a passion
> As love doth give my heart...
> Orsino, Act 2, Scene 4, 90-93

Orsino also makes some pretty mean comments about women not feeling love as strongly as men. He's proved wrong though. Shakespeare makes a woman, Viola, the model for true love in the play.

At the end of the play everyone gets married — a standard happy ending for a comedy. But Feste sings a sad song when the other characters have left the stage. All the way through the play is the idea that youth and love don't last long.

> Then come kiss me, sweet and twenty;
> Youth's a stuff will not endure.
> Feste, Act 2, Scene 3, 48-49

What's love got to do with it? — Well, pretty much everything...

Shakespeare obviously watched a lot of daytime TV soaps to know so much about love. Comedies almost always involved a lot of lovin' — and Twelfth Night is no exception.

Things Aren't What They Seem

A lot of the funny moments in _Twelfth Night_ are when the characters don't really understand what's happening to them. They think one thing, but something else is true — nothing's what it seems.

You Can't Trust The Way Things Look in the Play

Everybody's acting out of character and on top of that you've got Viola dressed up as a man who looks exactly like Sebastian.

It's hardly surprising people get confused — even Feste the jester:

> ...Nothing that is so, is so.
> Act 4, Scene 1, 7

You Can't See the Truth About Anyone Else

People can look like one person and be another.
The biggest misunderstanding in the play is over Viola.
Everybody except the Captain believes she's a man.

Even objects can be fake — like the letter Malvolio finds, which looks like it's been written by Olivia.

Olivia makes a whopping mistake about Viola.
She thinks Cesario is wonderful and falls in love — but she doesn't realise Cesario/Viola is actually a woman.

I'm sorry, I thought you were a bloke. But, let's face it, you are a bit mannish.

Antonio gets muddled by Viola too. Viola looks like Sebastian, so Antonio assumes she is Sebastian and gets cross with her for betraying his friendship:

> Will you deny me now?
> Act 3, Scene 4, 316

Antonio and Olivia are judging on appearances — they think that because someone looks beautiful, they're good.
But the whole play's about the fact that appearances can be deceiving.

Viola understands that appearances can be misleading:

> nature with a beauteous wall
> Doth oft close in pollution, Act 1, Scene 2, 48-9

"a beauteous wall" = beautiful appearance
"pollution" = evil

A lot of the characters seem to have strong feelings, but those feelings aren't always genuine.

Orsino swears he's in love with Olivia through most of the play.
But at the end of the play, he's happy to marry Viola — he knows her much better.

Olivia says she'll mourn her brother for seven years and won't even think about marriage in that time.
As soon as she meets Cesario, she changes her mind.

What a ridiculous plot — that'd never happen in real life...

When you're reading the play look out for characters misunderstanding who people are and what they're like. Knowing this stuff will show the examiner you really know your _Twelfth Night_ onions.

Viola Confuses Everyone

OK, time to own up — there are two really <u>dodgy bits</u> in the story of *Twelfth Night*.
One is that Viola <u>dresses up</u> as a <u>man</u>, the other is that she looks <u>exactly like</u> Sebastian.

Viola Pretends to Be a Man

This is one of those things that can seem really <u>odd</u> to us.
It's the <u>only way</u> for the story to work — so you've just got to <u>accept</u> it.

> Well, it says here that your hobbies include watching football, drinking beer and leaving the toilet seat up. Is that right?

> (High girly voice)... Yes..., I mean (deep manly voice)... yes, Duke. And I really hate shopping, too.

1) <u>Don't worry</u> too much about <u>why</u> Viola dresses up as a man. The <u>main reason</u> is that Shakespeare thought it would <u>make</u> his audience <u>laugh</u>. It's a bit like <u>pantomimes</u> — you often get a <u>woman</u> playing the part of the <u>male hero</u>.

2) There's a <u>practical reason</u> for Viola pretending to be a man — it helps her to <u>find a job</u> and a <u>place to live</u> in a country where she's a <u>stranger</u>. It'd be much more <u>difficult</u> and <u>dangerous</u> for a woman on her own.

3) It would have seemed <u>funnier</u> in <u>Shakespeare's time</u>. Women <u>never</u> wore the same clothes as men, and were expected to behave <u>very differently</u>.

Sebastian Doubles the Confusion

Because Viola's dressed like a man, she <u>looks</u> exactly like her brother.
She even says she's <u>based</u> her male outfit on her brother:

> <u>Everyone else</u> thinks that Sebastian and Viola/Cesario are the <u>same person</u>.

> and he went
> Still in this fashion, colour, ornament,
> For him I imitate.
> Act 3, Scene 4, 351-353

Learn This Bit Now — It Tells You Who Does What

It's seriously <u>confusing</u> — and very <u>unrealistic</u>. Make sure you learn <u>these</u> bits.
Sorry, folks, but it's the <u>only way</u> there is to make it less confusing.

Act 3, Scene 4
Antonio rescues <u>Viola/Cesario</u> from the fight with Sir Andrew — but then he gets <u>arrested</u>. Antonio asks for the <u>money</u> he gave <u>Sebastian</u> earlier, but <u>Viola/Cesario</u> <u>doesn't know</u> what he's talking about. Antonio <u>thinks</u> Sebastian has <u>betrayed</u> him.

Act 4, Scene 1
<u>Sir Andrew</u> and <u>Sir Toby</u> try to fight <u>Sebastian</u>, thinking he's Cesario. Olivia comes in and is <u>furious</u> with Sir Toby for fighting Cesario. Olivia takes <u>Sebastian</u> home, and in *Scene 3* they <u>marry</u>. <u>Sebastian</u> thinks she's gorgeous so he <u>goes along</u> with it all, even though he's <u>suspicious</u> — he <u>can't believe</u> his luck.

Act 5, Scene 1
<u>Viola</u>'s in <u>big trouble</u> because a lot of people <u>think</u> she's Sebastian.
1) <u>Antonio</u> accuses Viola/Cesario of being an <u>unfaithful friend</u>.
2) <u>Olivia</u> accuses Viola/Cesario of <u>denying</u> being her <u>husband</u>.
3) <u>Orsino</u> accuses Viola/Cesario of <u>betraying him</u> by <u>marrying</u> Olivia.
4) <u>Sir Andrew</u> accuses Viola/Cesario of <u>hurting</u> Sir Toby and him in a <u>fight</u>.

Oh ho ho — the laughs...

<u>Everybody</u> falls for Viola's <u>disguise</u> — I told you that comedy <u>doesn't</u> have to be <u>realistic</u>.

Fools

Twelfth Night is full of people <u>making fools</u> of themselves — it's one of the <u>big ideas</u> in the play. There's even a <u>professional</u> Fool. Fun fun fun.

Feste's a *Fool* — but he's *Not Stupid*

In many of Shakespeare's plays, <u>kings</u> or <u>rich people</u> have a <u>Fool</u>.
The Fool is <u>paid</u> to be idiotic — he's a <u>professional clown</u>, paid to <u>make</u> people <u>laugh</u>.
<u>Feste</u> is <u>Olivia's Fool</u>, but he also entertains <u>Orsino</u>.

1) A Fool was <u>allowed</u> to <u>make jokes</u> about <u>anything</u> — Feste even <u>takes the mickey</u> out of Orsino and Olivia. Because he's funny he <u>doesn't</u> have to live by the <u>same rules</u> as everyone else.

> There is no slander in an allowed fool
> though he do nothing but rail;
> Act 1, Scene 5, 82-83

2) He's one of the <u>only characters</u> who <u>understands</u> that everything has gone <u>crazy</u> in the play. It seems like <u>everyone else</u> is <u>behaving</u> like a Fool as well. He <u>tells</u> most of the characters this to their faces.

> This fellow is wise enough to play the fool,
> And to do that well craves a kind of wit;
> Act 3, Scene 1, 54-55

3) His jokes are all based on <u>wordplay</u> (see page 28) — he <u>twists</u> what people say to give it <u>another meaning</u>. That takes <u>brains</u> — Viola recognises how <u>clever</u> Feste really is.

4) Feste's a <u>singer</u> as well as a joker. His songs <u>aren't</u> meant to be funny. They're to <u>remind</u> people that love and happiness <u>don't last</u> (page 22).

Fooling *Can Also Mean* Playing Tricks

Clever <u>practical jokes</u> were part of the Feast of Fools celebrations (see page 13). They're part of *Twelfth Night* too.

Maria plants the <u>fake letter</u> for Malvolio to read in order to <u>make a fool</u> of him. She makes him think Olivia is in love with him, and tells him to <u>dress up</u> in a silly costume and <u>act strangely</u>.

Sir Andrew is Just *Plain Foolish*

Sir Andrew <u>isn't trying</u> to be a fool, although he sometimes tries to be <u>funny</u>. Foolishness <u>isn't</u> a <u>temporary</u> madness for him, he really is a <u>stupid fool</u>.

...And he asked for two slices of brown toast.

I don't get it. But I'd better laugh anyway or I'll look stupid.

1) Sir Andrew <u>never understands</u> what's going on, and <u>can't keep up</u> with the jokes.

2) Sir Toby is always <u>teasing</u> him — Toby just wants to <u>get money</u> out of him.

3) According to Maria his talents are "<u>most natural</u>". A "<u>natural</u>" was another word for somebody <u>born</u> a bit <u>simple</u>.

When clowns eat too much they say "No more, I'm fool"...

There are <u>three</u> types of fooling to learn about here — Feste's <u>wordplay</u>, Sir Andrew's <u>natural</u> foolishness, and <u>playing tricks</u> on people. It's one of the big <u>themes</u> in the play — so pay attention.

The End of the Play

At the <u>end</u> of the play the confusion is all <u>cleared up</u> — and everyone gets married.
But it <u>isn't</u> a happy ending for everyone...

Most of the Characters Get What They Deserve

<u>Viola</u>'s been loyal to Orsino, and ends up marrying him.

<u>Olivia</u> is married to Sebastian, not Cesario.

<u>Sebastian</u> and <u>Viola</u> are reunited.

<u>Sir Toby</u> and <u>Sir Andrew</u> have been drunk and disorderly and get beaten up by Sebastian.

For <u>most</u> of the play people have been behaving in <u>unexpected</u> ways,
but at the end the <u>normal rules</u> come back into force.

<u>Orsino</u> gives up his exaggerated feelings for Olivia,
and decides to marry his real friend Viola.

<u>Viola</u> gives up her disguise as a man.

<u>Olivia</u> snaps out of the spell cast by Cesario. She finally sorts out her
household — and gets to the bottom of the trick played on Malvolio.

The <u>main characters</u> get <u>married</u> — that's how Shakespeare's comedies <u>always</u>
<u>end</u>. <u>Orsino</u> marries <u>Viola</u>, <u>Sebastian</u> marries <u>Olivia</u> and <u>Sir Toby</u> marries <u>Maria</u>.

But Not Everyone Ends Up Happy

At the end of <u>*Twelfth Night*</u> there are a few things which <u>spoil</u> the happy ending.

Malvolio is <u>furious</u> when he finds out he's been tricked.
He storms out threatening <u>revenge</u>:

I'll be revenged on the whole pack of you!
Act 5, Scene 1, 362

<u>Feste's song</u> at the very end of the play makes him sound
<u>sick</u> of fooling. It really feels like the party's <u>over</u>.

You never find out <u>what happens</u> to <u>Antonio</u>.

Oh dear. I seem to have arrived a little early. Could you just stand there, please. The steamroller is on its way.

Are you sure this happens to me? I think you've got the wrong script.

This Play Doesn't Just Make People Laugh

The atmosphere of <u>*Twelfth Night*</u> is very strange. It's meant to be a comedy,
but there are lots of <u>sad moments</u> alongside the bits that make you laugh.

All Feste's <u>songs</u> remind you that
<u>real life</u> is <u>sad</u>, and <u>happiness</u>
is only a <u>passing thing</u>.

The <u>trick</u> played on Malvolio is <u>meant</u> to be fun, but it
gets very <u>nasty</u>. Even Sir Toby's <u>sick</u> of it by the end.
You start to <u>feel sorry</u> for Malvolio <u>instead</u> of laughing.

And everyone lives happily ever after — almost...

You could easily get <u>asked</u> to write about the <u>last scene</u>, so you need to know why it's a <u>happy</u>
<u>ending</u> for <u>some</u> characters and a <u>sad ending</u> for <u>others</u>. Watch out for <u>sad bits</u> in <u>other scenes</u> too.

Revision Summary

Twelfth Night is a tricky old play — but it's still possible to understand it. Grit your teeth, hold your nose and take a deep breath — then have a go at these questions before you explode. They're here for practice, so don't bother cheating. Work through them all without looking back over the section. Then if there's anything you're still not sure about, go back and have another look.

1) Where is the play set?

2) Does *Twelfth Night* show a realistic view of that country?

3) Is it likely that Shakespeare had visited the place where the play is set?

4) What role did nobles have in Elizabethan England?

5) What job does Malvolio do in Olivia's house?

6) What gets broken in *Twelfth Night*:
   a) the rules of good playwriting,   b) the rules of society,   c) Sir Andrew's glasses?

7) Explain what the Feast of Fools was.

8) What makes the characters act strangely in the play?

9) In the 1600s who was more powerful in society — men or women?

10) What is Courtly Love?

11) What kind of love does Olivia feel for Cesario?

12) Complete this sentence: *Twelfth Night* has a plot based on...
    a) ...misunderstanding and coincidence.
    b) ...crime and punishment.
    c) ...bacon and eggs.

13) Is Olivia right to judge by appearances, when she meets Cesario? Why?

14) Why do Sir Andrew and Sir Toby fight Sebastian?

15) Name four people who get angry with Viola because of the confusion with her brother.

16) Write down the two meanings of the word "fool".

17) Who does Sebastian marry? Who does Viola marry? Who does Sir Toby marry?

18) What happens to Malvolio at the end of the play?

19) Give two examples of sad bits in the play.

...and when the music stops, marry the person on your left.

Who's Who in the Play

There are loads of characters in the play, with all sorts of tricky names. The main ones are on this page. It's easy to get muddled — so go through this carefully.

Olivia's Household

SIR ANDREW AGUECHEEK

friend of Sir Toby

SIR TOBY BELCH

a relative of Olivia's living at her house

OLIVIA

wealthy Countess

MARIA

gentlewoman, attendant on Olivia

FABIAN

servant

MALVOLIO

steward — organises house and servants

FESTE

Feste officially works for Olivia, but he sometimes works at Orsino's too.

Viola & Sebastian

VIOLA
disguised as
CESARIO

SEBASTIAN

Viola's twin brother

Orsino's Household

DUKE ORSINO

ruler of Illyria

VALENTINE

attendant on Orsino

CURIO

attendant on Orsino

ANTONIO

friend of Sebastian, rescues him from shipwreck

Olivia and Orsino — they're household names...

Shakespeare gave his characters some weird old names. Use this page to learn the names and who's related to who. It'll make things one heck of a lot easier in the long run.

Orsino

Don't let these funny names put you off — Shakespeare just stuck them in to make the play sound more exotic. The important thing is to learn what sort of people the characters are.

Orsino Rules Illyria

Orsino is a Duke. He's the ruler of Illyria — the chief noble.

In the play, he doesn't do much ruling. He's too busy being in love with Olivia to worry about running the country.

He's rich, he speaks nicely and he's probably handsome. But he's a bit wet too — instead of going to see Olivia himself, he sends other people, right up until the very end of the play.

He's Terribly In Love with Olivia

1) You see Orsino in the first scene of the play. In every scene he's in, he moans about how much he's in love and that it's impossible for him to think about anything else.

Baby, you're irresistible.

2) He never seems to ask himself what Olivia wants — he just assumes he'll win her over in the end.

3) Orsino is sure he's the most in love that anyone's ever been. He's especially sure that his feelings are much deeper than any woman's could be:

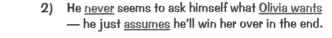

> There is no woman's sides
> Can bide the beating of so strong a passion
> As love doth give my heart...
> Act 2, Scene 4, 90-92

4) At the end of the play he finds out he was wrong. The person who loves him most deeply is Viola/Cesario — and she's a woman.

Orsino Snaps Out Of It in the End

At the end of the play Orsino has two big surprises.

Er...I'm not sure you'll like this one.

A surprise? By golly, I love surprises!

> The first one's a mistake. He thinks that Cesario has married Olivia behind his back.

The second one is real. He finds out that Cesario's a woman called Viola. He realises that she loves him and has been loyal, and asks her to marry him.

The Duke wins an award — a nobel prize...

If you get asked about Orsino, it'll be about love. The thing to remember is that he enjoys the idea of being in love with Olivia, but he doesn't really know what love is till the end of the play.

Viola

You really need to <u>learn</u> what <u>Viola's like</u> — she's the <u>key character</u> in the <u>love story</u>.
She falls in love with <u>Orsino</u> and Olivia falls in love with <u>her</u> — it's nice to be popular, I guess.

Viola's New in Illyria

1) Viola and her brother Sebastian are from a town called <u>Messaline</u>.

2) They're on a voyage but they get <u>shipwrecked</u>. Viola ends up in <u>Illyria</u>, thinking that Sebastian has <u>drowned</u>.

3) She has to decide <u>what to do</u>, and how she's going to <u>look after herself</u> in a country where she's a <u>complete stranger</u>.

She Disguises Herself as a Boy to Get a Job

<u>Duke Orsino</u> is somebody Viola's heard her <u>father</u> mention in the <u>past</u>.
She decides to <u>dress up as a man</u>, and see if she can get a <u>place</u> serving <u>Orsino</u>.

> Don't forget — Viola calls herself Cesario.
> Be careful not to get confused.

Orsino decides to send her as a <u>messenger</u> to tell
Olivia how much <u>he loves her</u>. Unfortunately, Viola
soon realises <u>she's</u> fallen in love with Orsino <u>herself</u>:

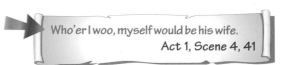

Who'er I woo, myself would be his wife.
Act 1, Scene 4, 41

Viola's Pretty Chilled Out — She Goes with the Flow

When everything starts getting complicated in the play, Viola <u>doesn't hurry</u> to <u>sort things out</u>.
She <u>waits</u> to see how things will go, and she <u>doesn't reveal</u> her secret till the end of the play.

When Viola realises Olivia's <u>in love</u> with her,
she decides to <u>wait and see</u> what happens.
She <u>doesn't</u> tell Olivia she's a woman.

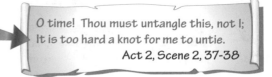

O time! Thou must untangle this, not I;
It is too hard a knot for me to untie.
Act 2, Scene 2, 37-38

Even when Sir Toby is trying to make her <u>fight</u> Sir Andrew, she <u>doesn't</u>
give away her <u>secret</u>. Luckily for her, she gets <u>rescued</u> by Antonio.

Dressing up as a boy — breeches the rules a bit...

Viola's a dead <u>important character</u>. You've really got to get to grips with <u>what she's like</u>, and how
she <u>deals</u> with her <u>weird situation</u>. <u>Learn</u> the stuff on this page and you'll be well on your way.

Sebastian

Sebastian <u>doesn't</u> appear as often as his sister. But when he does, he really gets things <u>moving</u>.
Make sure you know what he's like — if he appears in a scene, there's usually <u>trouble</u>.

Sebastian is Viola's Twin Brother

They look <u>amazingly similar</u>, which is where the problems start.

It's <u>especially</u> confusing because Viola wears clothes just like her <u>brother's</u>.

> ...he went
> Still in this fashion, colour, ornament,
> For him I imitate.
> *Act 3, Scene 4, 351-353*

For Viola and Sebastian to look so <u>similar</u> they must be quite <u>young</u>. Sebastian can't exactly be a <u>strapping great lad</u> with stubble.

NEXT!!!

Auditioning today for *SEBASTIAN*

He Gets Saved *from the* Shipwreck

In Act 2 we find out Sebastian was <u>rescued</u> by <u>Antonio</u>.
He stays with Antonio for about <u>three months</u>, before he heads for <u>Orsino's court</u>.

Sebastian thinks Viola <u>drowned</u> in the wreck. He's <u>gutted</u> that he won't see her again:

> She is drowned already, sir, with salt water, though
> I seem to drown her remembrance again with more.
> *Act 2, Scene 1, 25-27*

He's saying he's <u>drowning</u> her <u>memory</u> with <u>more salt water</u> in his tears.

Sebastian's Got More Get Up and Go *than his Sister*

1)   As soon as Sebastian arrives in town he's eager to go off and <u>see the sights</u>.

2)   When Sir Andrew and Sir Toby <u>attack him</u> in Act 4, Scene 1, he's happy to <u>fight back</u>.

3)   When Olivia <u>invites</u> him to her house, he goes with her.

4)   He realises it's a <u>weird</u> situation, but he really fancies Olivia, so he's happy to <u>go along</u> with it even though he thinks it's crazy:

> ...I am mad,
> Or else the lady's mad...
> *Act 4, Scene 3, 15-16*

5)   In Act 5, Scene 1, Sebastian apologises to Olivia for beating up Sir Toby <u>and</u> Sir Andrew. They <u>were</u> both drunk, but it's still quite impressive to win a fight against <u>two</u> grown men.

Maggot twins — they always go round in pears...

Sebastian gets important in Act 4, where everyone starts <u>mistaking</u> him for Viola/Cesario. You need to know <u>how different</u> he is from Viola — he's <u>happy to fight</u> and he <u>loves Olivia</u>... She <u>doesn't</u>.

Olivia

Olivia's the <u>object</u> of Orsino's love — but she falls for <u>Viola/Cesario</u>.
She starts off as a <u>sad figure</u>, but ends up looking pretty <u>silly</u>.

Olivia's a *Beautiful Countess*

1) Olivia lives in the same town as Orsino. She's a <u>Countess</u>
   so she's part of the same <u>social circle</u> as Duke Orsino.

2) Olivia's <u>father</u> and <u>brother</u> have <u>died</u> recently.
   She's the heir to the family house and money.

3) When her brother died Olivia swore to <u>shut herself away</u> from
   the world. She is so <u>sad</u> that she plans to wear a <u>veil</u> and
   stay in her house for <u>seven years</u>, grieving for her brother.

She's a *Powerful Person*

Olivia's <u>in charge</u> of her household — <u>even</u> her uncle Sir Toby Belch.
She has to <u>keep</u> everyone in <u>order</u>, calmly and fairly.

In Act 1, Scene 5, <u>Feste</u> and <u>Malvolio</u> start bickering. Malvolio <u>insults</u> Feste's
fooling, and Olivia has to break up the argument. She tells Malvolio <u>exactly</u> what
<u>she thinks</u> of his attitude:

> *O you are sick of self-love, Malvolio...*
> Act 1, Scene 5, 79

Later in the <u>same scene</u> she tells
Feste to <u>behave himself</u> too:

> *Now you see, sir, how your fooling grows
> old, and people dislike it.*
> Act 1, Scene 5, 98-99

When She *Falls in Love* She *Falls Apart*

Olivia falls in love with Viola/Cesario almost as <u>soon</u> as she <u>sees</u> him.
She <u>forgets</u> everything else immediately.

It's as if she's gone <u>mad</u> — all she cares about is seeing Viola/Cesario again.
To the audience, she's making a <u>fool</u> of herself because Viola/Cesario is really a <u>girl</u>.

She <u>loses track</u> of what's <u>going on</u> in her household. She <u>doesn't realise</u> Malvolio's been <u>tricked</u> in Act 3
Scene 4 — she thinks he's <u>gone mad</u> and lets <u>Toby</u> deal with the problem, and it all gets <u>out of hand</u>.

> She <u>marries Sebastian</u> thinking he's Cesario —
> she only <u>discovers</u> her <u>mistake</u> at the <u>end</u> of the play.

The round table — that was a social circle...

Olivia's a <u>sad</u> and <u>serious</u> figure at the <u>start</u> of the play, but she ends up looking <u>daft</u> because she
falls in love with a <u>girl</u>. Remember — the trick on Malvolio <u>only</u> works because she's <u>distracted</u>.

Malvolio

Malvolio's a <u>weird</u> character — in the <u>early part</u> of the play you want to <u>hate</u> him, and it's <u>funny</u> watching him fall for Maria's <u>trick</u>. But by the <u>end</u> of the play you can't help feeling <u>sorry</u> for him.

Malvolio *is Olivia's Steward*

1) His job is to <u>manage Olivia's house</u>.
He's her <u>chief</u> servant — a responsible job.

2) Malvolio takes his job <u>really seriously</u>, and he's always telling people <u>what to do</u>. The way he does it is really <u>annoying</u> though — he's got <u>no</u> sense of humour and he's very <u>rude</u> and <u>bossy</u>.

3) <u>Everyone</u> apart from Olivia <u>hates</u> Malvolio. In Act 1, Scene 5, he <u>insults</u> Feste's fooling:

> I marvel your ladyship takes delight in such a barren rascal.
> Act 1, Scene 5, 72-73

4) In Act 2, Scene 3, Malvolio <u>storms in</u> when Feste, Sir Toby and Sir Andrew are drinking and singing late at night, disturbing everyone. He <u>insults</u> them and <u>threatens</u> to tell Olivia that <u>Maria</u> gave them wine.

> My masters, are you mad?
> Act 2, Scene 3, 80

> she shall know of it, by this hand.
> Act 2, Scene 3, 115

Maria *Tricks Him in Revenge*

She writes a <u>love-letter</u> to Malvolio that <u>looks</u> like it comes from <u>Olivia</u>. It tells Malvolio to do all sorts of <u>stupid things</u> to <u>prove</u> his love for her.

Even better, Malvolio is so arrogant that he <u>already</u> thinks that Olivia fancies him. When he finds the letter, he's <u>convinced</u> Olivia loves him madly:

> for every reason excites to this, that my lady loves me.
> Act 2, Scene 5, 145

At the *End You Start Feeling Sorry For Him*

1) In Act 3, Scene 4, Malvolio appears in front of Olivia with a <u>big smile</u> and a <u>silly outfit</u>, and it's still very <u>funny</u>. Unfortunately, Olivia thinks he <u>really is</u> mad. She says Sir Toby should <u>look after</u> him. This is where the story takes a <u>nasty</u> turn.

2) Sir Toby and Maria <u>lock him up</u> as though he <u>really is</u> mad. They keep him away from Olivia so he's got <u>no chance</u> to defend himself. They send <u>Feste</u> to him <u>pretending</u> to be a <u>priest</u> — just to <u>make fun</u> of him even more.

It's a really <u>unpleasant ending</u> for the comedy story.

3) Even Sir Toby realises the joke's gone <u>too far</u>, but he <u>doesn't know</u> what he can do about it. When Malvolio finally gets out, he's <u>furious</u> with Olivia. After he finds out about the trick, he rushes off promising <u>revenge</u> on everyone.

Malvolio — sounds like a sick Italian rodent...

Malvolio's one of the <u>hardest</u> characters to <u>write about</u>. You need to be careful with which scene you write about — in the <u>early scenes</u> he's really <u>horrible</u> but by the end you <u>feel sorry</u> for him.

Sir Toby and Sir Andrew

These two <u>start off</u> as the <u>comic relief</u> in the play — but they <u>end up</u> getting their <u>just desserts</u> for all the trouble they cause.

Sir Toby Belch is a Self-Centred Sponger

He's Olivia's <u>uncle</u> — but he's living in her house because he has <u>no money</u> of his own. He's also <u>sponging money</u> off <u>Sir Andrew</u>, by telling him that Olivia will <u>marry him</u>.

1) Even though he lives in Olivia's house, he <u>refuses</u> to live by her rules:

> I'll confine myself no finer than I am:
> Act 1, Scene 3, 8

2) He thinks Olivia's <u>being stupid</u> to mourn her brother's death.

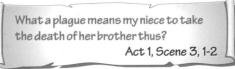

> What a plague means my niece to take the death of her brother thus?
> Act 1, Scene 3, 1-2

3) As if that wasn't bad enough, he spends <u>almost all</u> of the play <u>drunk</u>.

4) Sir Toby <u>hates</u> Malvolio and <u>enjoys</u> the trick played on him. He <u>takes the mickey</u> out of Sir Andrew all the time and <u>forces</u> him to <u>challenge</u> Viola/Cesario to a duel just for a <u>laugh</u>.

5) At the end of the play we're told he's <u>married Maria</u>. The <u>last</u> time he comes on stage is after he and Andrew have been <u>beaten up</u> by Sebastian. He's <u>not</u> a funny character any more, and he turns on Andrew and tells him <u>exactly</u> what he <u>really thinks</u> of him.

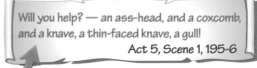

> Will you help? — an ass-head, and a coxcomb, and a knave, a thin-faced knave, a gull!
> Act 5, Scene 1, 195-6

> <u>Sir Toby</u> and <u>Sir Andrew</u> are definitely <u>not heroic</u>, even though they're <u>knights</u>.

Sir Andrew Aguecheek Just Doesn't Get It

1) Sir Andrew's a bit <u>thick</u> — he doesn't really know what's going on. He <u>tries</u> to join in with Sir Toby and Feste's <u>witty jokes</u>, but he <u>can't</u> quite manage it.

2) Sir Toby is <u>only</u> friends with him because of his <u>money</u>, and so that he can <u>laugh</u> at him — Andrew doesn't <u>stand a chance</u> with Olivia but he doesn't <u>realise</u> it.

3) Sir Andrew is <u>cowardly</u> but very <u>funny</u>. Even though he's <u>silly</u>, there's a moment when you realise that <u>deep down</u> he might be <u>decent</u>, if only Sir Toby weren't <u>controlling</u> him:

> He's a <u>sad</u> figure as well — <u>none</u> of his friends are <u>real</u>. They're only <u>using</u> him.

> I was adored once too.
> Act 2, Scene 3, 167

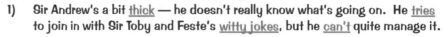

An evening with Sir Toby — a good knight out...

Sir Toby is a <u>brilliant character</u>. You might need to mention him because he turns up a lot in the play. You've got to know what makes him tick — <u>other people's money</u>, <u>wine</u> and <u>laughter</u>.

Feste

Almost <u>everything</u> Feste says is a <u>joke</u>, or a <u>play on words</u>. He's <u>not</u> really a character in his own right — he's more of a <u>commentator</u> on what happens.

It's Feste's Job to Make People Laugh

1) Feste's a <u>professional Fool</u> or Clown. It's his job to entertain people by <u>joking</u> and <u>singing</u>.

2) He's <u>allowed</u> to make jokes about <u>anything</u> he wants to — even if it's dead <u>offensive</u>.

> There is no slander in an allowed fool
> Act 1, Scene 5, 82

3) He's the <u>only character</u> who can say what he <u>really thinks</u> of everyone else. He jokingly tells Olivia that she's a fool for grieving so much for her brother.

His jokes are based on <u>puns</u> and <u>wordplay</u> — see page 34.

> Good madonna, give me leave to prove you a fool.
> Act 1, Scene 5, 50

He's in it for the Money

Feste's <u>supposed</u> to be <u>Olivia's</u> Fool, but he's happy to go wherever the <u>money</u> is.

He sings <u>sad songs</u> for <u>Orsino</u> when the Duke's feeling melancholy, but he also sings <u>sad love songs</u> for <u>Sir Toby</u> and <u>Sir Andrew</u> when they're drunk.

He <u>jokes</u> with people to <u>make money</u> too — with <u>Viola/Cesario</u> in Act 3, Scene 1; with <u>Sebastian</u> in Act 4, Scene 1; and with <u>Orsino</u> in Act 5, Scene 1.

The <u>only</u> time Feste <u>isn't worried</u> about <u>money</u> is when he pretends to be a priest for the trick on <u>Malvolio</u>.

Feste Really Hates Malvolio

Feste is <u>livid</u> at what Malvolio says about him in Act 1, Scene 5. It's a really <u>harsh criticism</u> of his skills.

At the <u>end of the play</u>, Feste tells Malvolio he was involved in the trick, and almost quotes what Malvolio said to him (see page 25).

> But do you remember — 'Madam, why laugh you at such a barren rascal, and you smile not, he's gagged'?
> Act 5, Scene 1, 358-360

Feste <u>only</u> got involved in the trick to get his <u>revenge</u> on Malvolio.

Melon-collie — is that a fruity kind of dog...

It's ridiculous to think that you can make a living from writing puns. Pathetic. Anyway, Feste's an odd character — you <u>never</u> really get to know him. He's only important in the way that he <u>relates</u> to the <u>other characters</u> in the play. Remember — his job is to make <u>jokes</u> and <u>entertain</u>.

Maria and Fabian

Blimey — these characters keep on coming. <u>Maria</u> and <u>Fabian</u> are important for the <u>Malvolio story</u>.

Maria's the <u>Brains Behind the Trick</u> on Malvolio

Maria is Olivia's <u>gentlewoman</u> — her personal attendant.

Maria's <u>good friends</u> with <u>Sir Toby</u>. In Act 1, Scene 3, she <u>warns him</u> that Olivia <u>isn't happy</u> with his behaviour, and tells him that Sir Andrew is a <u>worthless fool</u>.

In Act 1, Scene 5, she <u>warns Feste</u> that Olivia's cross with him for disappearing. He's sharp enough to spot that <u>she</u> and <u>Sir Toby</u> should <u>get together</u>.

> ...if Sir Toby would leave drinking, thou wert as witty a piece of Eve's flesh as any in Illyria.
> Act 1, Scene 5, 23-25

She's <u>furious</u> with Malvolio when he <u>tells her off</u> for giving Toby and Andrew wine in Act 2, Scene 3 — but because he's the <u>chief</u> servant, she <u>can't</u> answer him back. That's when she decides to get her <u>revenge</u> by writing the <u>fake love letter</u>.

Maria <u>doesn't appear</u> in the last scene of the play, but Fabian says that <u>Sir Toby</u> has <u>married</u> her.

Fabian <u>Works for Olivia</u> too

Fabian is <u>another</u> member of Olivia's <u>household</u>.
He's got a <u>grudge</u> against Malvolio too so he <u>joins in</u> with the <u>trick</u>.

1) Fabian says he's <u>glad</u> to be part of the trick on Malvolio because Malvolio got him in <u>trouble</u> with <u>Olivia</u> for organising a <u>bear-baiting</u> at the house:

> You know he brought me out o' favour with my lady about a bear-baiting here.
> Act 2, Scene 5, 6-7

2) He also helps Sir Toby <u>wind up</u> Sir Andrew and Viola/Cesario before their duel.

3) In the <u>last</u> scene, he's a lot <u>more serious</u> — when Olivia offers to let Malvolio investigate who played the trick, Fabian <u>confesses</u> everything.

4) He <u>says</u> it was <u>Toby</u> and <u>he</u> who planned it — but actually <u>Maria did</u>. He tries to say it was all just a <u>joke</u>, but that there were <u>good reasons</u> for it on <u>both sides</u>.

> How with a sportful malice it was followed
> May rather pluck on laughter than revenge,
> Act 5, Scene 1, 350-51

Fabian has a grudge — sounds painful...

Fabian and Maria <u>aren't</u> in many scenes, but you <u>can't ignore</u> them. If you write about any of the scenes about the trick they'll be there, so you'll need to know <u>why</u> they <u>hate</u> Malvolio.

Antonio and Others

Here's the last lot of characters to get to know, so get stuck in.

Antonio is Sebastian's Friend

Antonio's a sea-captain, and Sebastian's friend.

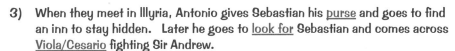

1) Antonio rescues Sebastian from the shipwreck.
    Sebastian stays with him for three months
    afterwards and they become good friends.

2) When Sebastian goes to Illyria, Antonio decides to
    follow him. Trouble is, Antonio was once involved in
    a battle with Orsino's ships. If he goes to Illyria he
    risks being arrested and executed.

3) When they meet in Illyria, Antonio gives Sebastian his purse and goes to find
    an inn to stay hidden. Later he goes to look for Sebastian and comes across
    Viola/Cesario fighting Sir Andrew.

4) He rescues her, thinking it's Sebastian, but he's arrested by the police. He
    asks for his purse and doesn't get it — he thinks Sebastian's betrayed him.

5) In Act 5, Scene 1, Antonio tells Orsino his story but no one believes him —
    it's only when Sebastian comes in that he's recognised. But even at the end
    of the play it's not clear whether he'll be let off or locked away.

The Other Characters Are Nothing to Worry About

There are a few other minor characters in the play.
You don't need to know much about them, just remember who they are.

1) The Captain of the wrecked ship is from Illyria.

    He's with Viola when she washes up on the shore, and helps
    her get to Orsino's court, and disguise herself as a man.

2) Curio and Valentine are
    attendants of Orsino.
    They don't get involved in
    the main story much.

3) There's a Priest
    who marries Olivia
    to Sebastian.

4) The two officers who arrest
    Antonio don't have time to
    show a personality. They just
    do their job then shuffle off.

On stage you could have extras too — lords at Orsino's
court, or sailors on the shore with Viola and the Captain.
That would be up to the director though.
You don't need them for the story to make sense.

Minor characters — I really dig them...

Good news — you don't need to know as much about these characters as about, say, Viola or Malvolio.
Just make sure you know who they are, in case you need to mention them in your essay.

Revision Summary

If you don't know who's who in the play it can get seriously confusing. You need to know the names of all the main characters — and how to spell them. What's more you've got to know what they're like, and the main events they get involved in. Keep going through these questions until you can answer them all without cheating. Answer them <u>all</u>, I said.

1) Who rules Illyria?

2) Who is he in love with?

3) What two surprises does he get at the end of the play?

4) Why does Viola dress up as a man?

5) What's Viola like? Does she:
   a) Mope around making everyone's life a misery?
   b) Try to sort everyone's problems out?
   c) Leave things to sort themselves out?

6) Whose brother is Sebastian?

7) What does he think happened to his sister?

8) Who saves Sebastian from the shipwreck?

9) Which two characters does Sebastian beat up?

10) Why is Olivia in mourning at the start of the play?

11) Who does Olivia fall in love with?

12) How does she behave when she's in love?

13) What's Malvolio's job?

14) Why does everyone find him so annoying?
    a) He steals money from Olivia.
    b) He doesn't approve of anyone having fun.
    c) He sings really badly and out of tune.

15) Whose idea is it to play a trick on Malvolio?

16) What relation is Sir Toby to Olivia?

17) Who's the thick one out of Sir Andrew and Sir Toby?

18) What's Feste's job?

19) Why does he work at Orsino's house as well as Olivia's house?

20) Why does Antonio get arrested?

21) Why does he ask Viola/Cesario for a purse?

Images In The Play

This play's full of <u>images</u> — some people say they're there to make the language <u>rich</u> and <u>interesting</u>. I think they just make it a lot <u>trickier to follow</u>, myself.

Learn *these* Three Kinds of Image to Look Out For

Images are just <u>word pictures</u> — they help you see what Shakespeare's describing.

① <u>Similes</u> are when one thing is <u>like</u> something else. They usually use "as or "like":

> as hungry as the sea
> Act 2, Scene 4, 97

> It is as fat and fulsome to mine ear
> As howling after music.
> Act 5, Scene 1, 102-103

They're a kind of <u>comparison</u> — and Shakespeare sticks them in all over the place.

② A <u>metaphor</u> is when he says one thing <u>is</u> something else. Usually it just means using <u>exaggerated language</u> to <u>describe</u> things.

Feste says time is a "<u>whirligig</u>" — a spinning top. He's basically saying "what goes around, comes around."

> And thus the whirligig of time brings in his revenges.
> Act 5, Scene 1, 360-1

Maria's using a <u>sailing</u> metaphor here to ask Viola/Cesario to leave.

> MARIA   Will you hoist sail, sir? Here lies your way.
> VIOLA   No, good swabber, I am to hull here a little longer.
>   Act 1, Scene 5, 182-183

Viola carries it on, calling Maria a "<u>swabber</u>" — a sailor who kept the decks of a ship clean — and saying she is "<u>to hull</u>" there. If a ship was "to hull", it was drifting without hoisting a sail. This <u>isn't</u> just pointless sailor talk — mentioning stuff like this in your exam <u>really helps</u> to prove to the examiner that you know what Shakespeare was talking about.

③ <u>Personification</u> means describing a thing <u>as if</u> it were a <u>person</u>.

> The clock upbraids me with the waste of time.
> Act 3, Scene 1, 123

The clock has just chimed — Olivia says it's <u>criticising</u> her for wasting time, <u>as if</u> it were a <u>person</u>.

This page is a light shining into your life... *(that's a metaphor)*

Spotting <u>different kinds</u> of image gets you <u>marks</u>, especially if you know the <u>fancy names</u>. So it's a good idea to learn exactly what <u>similes</u>, <u>metaphors</u> and <u>personification</u> are all about.

Common Images

Some images <u>turn up</u> time and again <u>all the way through</u> the play. In your essay you need to be able to spot images, and write about what they tell you about the play and the characters.

Look for Images Saying *Nothing Lasts Forever*

<u>Wasting time</u> is one of the big themes of the play — Shakespeare uses lots of different images to say that nothing lasts forever, so people should <u>seize the day</u>.

This song's all about how the future is <u>uncertain</u>, but youth <u>won't</u> last for ever — so people should <u>enjoy love here and now</u> before it's too late.

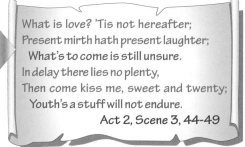

What is love? 'Tis not hereafter;
Present mirth hath present laughter;
  What's to come is still unsure.
In delay there lies no plenty,
Then come kiss me, sweet and twenty;
  Youth's a stuff will not endure.
          Act 2, Scene 3, 44-49

There are also lots of images of <u>flowers</u> describing <u>beauty</u> — saying it <u>doesn't last long</u>, like a flower.

beauty's a flower
        Act 1, Scene 5, 45

For women are as roses, whose fair flower,
Being once displayed, doth fall that very hour.
                    Act 2, Scene 4, 36-7

All these images are about <u>death</u> too — they're saying that once beauty is <u>gone</u>, it's dead <u>forever</u>.

And so they are. Alas, that they are so:
To die, even when they to perfection grow!
                  Act 2, Scene 4, 38-39

R.I.P.
BEAUTY

Watch For *Sea* and *Jewel* Images

The play is all about the effects of a <u>shipwreck</u>, and there are lots of <u>sea images</u>.

From the rude sea's enraged and foamy mouth
Did I redeem. A wrack past hope he was.
                      Act 5, Scene 1, 71-72

Antonio's talking about rescuing Sebastian from the sea <u>as if</u> Sebastian was a <u>wrecked ship</u> — a "<u>wrack past hope</u>".

thy mind is a very opal.
      Act 2, Scene 4, 71-72

There are also several images of <u>precious stones</u>:

Sea images — they've left me a wreck...

There are loads of <u>different images</u> in the play — this page is about some of the <u>most common</u> ones. Like the bits that say <u>nothing lasts forever</u>, or the stuff about the <u>sea</u> or <u>jewels</u>.

Section Four — Shakespeare's Language

Food Images

More important things to <u>learn</u> — this is a kind of image that you'll <u>keep on meeting</u> in the play. That means that <u>essays</u> about imagery in the play need to mention food images too.

The Play's Stuffed Full of Food Images

Right from the <u>opening line</u> the play uses a <u>food image</u>.

> If music be the food of love, play on —
> Give me excess of it, that, surfeiting,
> The appetite may sicken, and so die.
> Act 1, Scene 1, 1-3

Orsino's saying his love is like an <u>appetite</u>. He wants to <u>feed</u> it with so much <u>music</u> that he'll be <u>full</u> — and <u>won't feel</u> his love any more.

Later on, Orsino talks about love as an <u>appetite</u> again.

He's telling Viola/Cesario that women's love is <u>less strong</u> than men's because it's just an <u>appetite</u>.

> Alas, their love may be called appetite,
> No motion of the liver, but the palate,
> That suffers surfeit, cloyment and revolt;
> But mine is all as hungry as the sea,
> And can digest as much.
> Act 2, Scene 4, 94-98

He says his love is "as hungry as the sea" — it's <u>endlessly hungry</u>.

It's pretty much the <u>opposite</u> of what he said in Act 1 — Shakespeare's making it into a <u>joke</u> by having him use the <u>same image</u> in completely <u>different ways</u>.

When Valentine describes <u>Olivia's grief</u>, he uses a food image too.

> And water once a day her chamber round
> With eye-offending brine — all this to season
> A brother's dead love, which she would keep fresh
> And lasting, in her sad remembrance.
> Act 1, Scene 1, 29-32

Pickled Memories
in brine

<u>Brine</u> is salt water used to keep food <u>fresh</u>. Valentine's saying that Olivia's <u>salt-water tears</u> will keep her dead brother's love <u>fresh</u> in her memory.

Sir Toby uses a <u>food image</u> when he gets cross with Malvolio — "cakes and ale" are an image of <u>fun</u>.

> Art any more than a steward? Dost thou think, because thou art virtuous, there shall be no more cakes and ale?
> Act 2, Scene 3, 106-109

Sir Toby tells Malvolio that just because he's a goody-two-shoes <u>doesn't mean</u> that no one else can have any fun.

If music be the food of love — make mine Meatloaf...

Maybe Shakespeare was hungry at the time, or something. Whatever, eyes peeled for <u>food images</u>.

Puns and Wordplay

Twelfth Night is supposed to be a comedy — and it's packed full of jokes. Mind you, most of them aren't very funny — they're mostly based on words with <u>two meanings</u>.

Words **with** Double Meanings **are called** Puns

Shakespeare loved puns — his plays are <u>full</u> of them. They were really <u>popular</u> at the time he was writing, because everyone thought you were clever if you could make lots of puns.

> SIR TOBY   I mean, to go, sir, to enter.
> VIOLA   I will answer you with **gait** and **entrance** — but we are prevented.
>   Act 3, Scene 1, 75-77

Gait, like gate!
Ha ha ha ha ha, I'm so funny!

Sir Toby tells Viola to go and enter, so she makes a <u>pun</u> on the words "gait and entrance" meaning "going and entering", and "gate and entrance".

The Play's **Full** of this Wordplay

Feste calls himself a "corrupter of words" — part of his job is to find <u>double meanings</u> in words and phrases and <u>make jokes</u> about them.

> SIR ANDREW   Begin, fool. It begins, 'Hold thy peace.'
> FESTE   I shall never begin if I hold my **peace**.
>   Act 2, Scene 3, 63-64

Feste makes jokes about the word "<u>fool</u>" in several scenes.
He makes the <u>other characters</u> see that it can mean <u>many</u> different things.

> VIOLA   Art not thou the Lady Olivia's **fool**?
> FESTE   No, indeed, sir. The Lady Olivia has no folly. She will keep no **fool**, sir, till she be married.
>   Act 3, Scene 1, 27-29

The fool said <u>he'd</u> paid them!

Viola means a <u>professional fool</u> (a jester) — Feste says Olivia <u>won't</u> have a fool until she has a husband. He's saying that <u>all husbands</u> are <u>fools</u>.

Some **Double Meanings Cause** Misunderstandings

When Malvolio is trying to impress Olivia, he <u>doesn't understand</u> what she's really saying to him.

> OLIVIA   Wilt thou go to bed, Malvolio?
> MALVOLIO   To bed? Ay, sweetheart, and I'll come to thee.
>   Act 3, Scene 4, 28-9

He thinks she wants to sleep with him — in fact she's <u>worried</u> that he's sick.

Wordplay with cakes — all the current puns...

Even if you don't think Shakespeare's all that funny, you should be able to write about the <u>wordplay</u>. Be careful with anything <u>Feste says</u>, and look for <u>misunderstandings</u> like in Act 3, Scene 4.

Revision Summary

It may look like a cinch of a section at four pages, but it isn't a picnic. Or if it was, it would be a mouldy brown bread sandwich with a watery apple, while other people walk past eating lovely fat juicy chips... Mmmmm. But never fear, at least it's Shakespeare — a good looking bloke if ever I saw one. If he bunged in loads of imagery I'm sure he had a reason. Even if the only reason was to give you something to write about in essays.

1) Describe what a simile is.

2) What does Feste mean when he describes time as a "whirligig"?

3) When Maria says "Will you hoist sail, sir?" is she using a metaphor or a simile?

4) Give an example of personification from the play.

5) Write down a quote from the play saying that nothing lasts forever.

6) Is Feste's song in Act 2, Scene 3 happy or sad?

7) What does Shakespeare say about women's beauty in *Twelfth Night*?
    Give a quote from the play to back up your answer.

8) What key event in the story involves the sea?

9) Give two examples of food images in Orsino's speeches.

10) What is brine? What does Orsino mean when he says Olivia will water her
    bedroom with it?

11) What are "cakes and ale" an image of? Who talks about "cakes and ale"?

12) Complete this sentence: A pun is...
    a) ...a swear word
    b) ...a word with two meanings
    c) ...a lie.

13) Which character's job involves making puns?

14) Give three examples of wordplay in *Twelfth Night*. Explain the joke in each case.

The Play Has Two Stories

The play has two main plot lines — the love triangle and the trick played on Malvolio.

The Love Story

Romantic entanglements are the basis of the first plotline.
1) Viola is the main character — while pretending to be a bloke she falls in love with Orsino, and then Olivia falls in love with her.
2) The situation gets more complicated because Orsino is in love with Olivia, and also because Viola's twin brother Sebastian arrives who looks exactly like her.
3) It all ends happily — Viola marries Orsino and Olivia marries Sebastian.

The Malvolio Story

The second plotline is funny stuff about the less powerful people in Olivia's household.
1) Olivia's steward, Malvolio, gets annoyed when Sir Toby, Feste, Maria and Sir Andrew are having a party — so they decide to play a trick on him.
2) Maria decides that, because Malvolio is so vain, he would believe a fake love letter from Olivia — saying she fancies him and wants him to dress up for her.
3) Malvolio falls for the trick, which is pretty funny. It turns nasty though when the tricksters persuade Olivia to lock Malvolio up as a madman. He gets released in the end, but isn't happy.

The Two Storylines Contrast With Each Other

The character-types, language and attitudes to love in the two stories are very different.

In the LOVE STORY the people are a bit like those in a fairy story — they have exotic names and suffer for love. These characters belong in the fantasy world of Illyria. Shakespeare takes the mick out of them a bit though.

In the MALVOLIO STORY the people are a lot more down-to-earth. Sir Toby and Sir Andrew have English names and talk about pubs and pickled herring. They're a bit like the characters in a pantomine.

The characters in the love story talk in fancy, romantic language. Their lines are often written in poetry. These characters sometimes have soliloquies where they reveal their thoughts to the audience.

The characters in the Malvolio story speak much rougher language. A lot of their dialogue is bantering with a lot of rude insults, jokes and bad puns.

> Away before me to sweet beds of flowers —
> Love-thoughts lie rich when canopied with bowers.
> Orsino, Act 1, Scene 1, 40-41

> the niggardly, rascally sheep-biter
> Sir Toby, Act 2, Scene 5, 4-5

In the love story the characters have quite high ideals about what love should be like. Orsino reckons he feels true love for Olivia, and Viola really does feel it for him.

In the second story Sir Toby is much less romantic about love. He marries Maria because he likes her sense of humour.

> She sat like patience on a monument,
> Smiling at grief. Was not this love indeed?
> Viola, Act 2, Scene 4, 110-111

> I could marry this wench for this device —
> Sir Toby, Act 2, Scene 5, 160

Stagecraft — thespians in space...

Swapping the action backwards and forwards between two plot-lines stops the play getting boring. It's just like an episode of Eastenders, really. Yes, Eastenders is the Shakespeare of today...

How the Play is Structured

Shakespeare wasn't thick — the structure of *Twelfth Night* is really well thought out.

The Play is Carefully Structured

Twelfth Night has a complicated plot. Shakespeare had to find a way of telling the story
(i.e. structuring the play) that the audience would find funny and watchable. He had to decide:

a) What order to put the events in.

b) Which bits of the story were most important.

If you're asked to write about structure in your essay, think about why Shakespeare
chose that sequence of events and how he made important bits stand out.
Look for the comic and romantic highlights in the play.

Romantic build-up

— look at how the scenes are organised to create
emotional impact.

e.g. Act 1, Scene 2: Viola decides to dress as a boy and
become a servant of Orsino's
— this sets up the romantic situation.
Act 1, Scene 4: Viola adores Orsino, but he thinks
she's a bloke and wants her to chat up Olivia for him
— an emotional dilemma for Viola.
Act 2, Scene 4: Viola talks to Orsino about love,
and hints at how she feels
— a whole TV series worth of romantic tension.

Comic build-up

— look at how the play moves towards the
funniest situations.

e.g. Act 2, Scene 3: Malvolio annoys Maria
— a funny scene.
Act 2, Scene 5: Malvolio reads the trick letter
— a funnier scene.
Act 3, Scene 4: Malvolio wears silly clothes
— the funniest scene.

Focus on the Key Scenes

If every scene in the play was full of comic mayhem and romantic melodrama the audience
could get a bit cheesed off. It might sound weird, but a few boring scenes can make the best
bits of play stand out and seem even more brilliant.

So when you're writing about the play
try to focus on the key scenes where
the humour and emotion is at its peak.
It's fine to discuss minor scenes too
— but don't make them the main
subject of your essay.

The minor scenes in *Twelfth Night* often
help to set up the plot and prepare the
audience for the key scenes.

Key Scenes

Act 1, Scene 1 — Orsino's
palace sets the atmosphere.

Act 1, Scene 2 — Viola's
entrance kick-starts the story.

Act 1, Scene 4 — Viola, dressed as
a bloke, falls in love with Orsino.

Act 1, Scene 5 — Olivia falls in
love with Viola.

Act 2, Scene 4 — Orsino and Viola
discuss love = most emotional bit.

Act 2, Scene 5 — Malvolio falls
for the trick with the letter.

Act 3, Scene 4 — Malvolio
wears yellow stockings.
Sir Andrew nearly fights
Viola.

Act 4, Scene 1 —
Sebastian turns up,
confusing everyone.

Act 4, Scene 3 — Olivia
marries Sebastian.

Act 5, Scene 1 — The
confusion reaches its
height and then it all
gets sorted out.

It's a great play with lots of boring scenes — just what we like...

Thinking about key scenes is a good way to break the play down and understand it all. Putting
boring scenes in is another classic Eastenders trick (though they seem to forget to put in the good ones...)

Patterns in the Story

In some scenes it feels like <u>nothing much</u> is happening — but don't be fooled.
Shakespeare made sure that every bit of the play helped to <u>get the story across</u> to the audience.

Different *Scenes* do Different *Jobs*

Every scene is there for a <u>reason</u>. Scenes can do <u>different things</u>.

I'm not a plot device — I'm a free man!

1) Some scenes are just there to <u>move the plot forwards</u>, without much waffly talking. These scenes are usually really <u>short</u>.

> **Act 3, Scene 3** — Antonio turns up in Illyria and lends Sebastian his purse.

2) Some scenes are there to build up the <u>mood</u> of the play. Not much happens, but there's lots of <u>talking</u> and you find out more about what the characters <u>think</u>.

> **Act 2, Scene 4** — Orsino and Viola/Cesario rabbit on about love for ages. The play's about <u>love</u>, so Shakespeare tries to show the main characters' opinions about it.

3) And of course some scenes add to the mood <u>as well as</u> moving the plot on.

> **Act 4, Scene 3** — There's loads of moody poetry, but it's a really short scene — all that happens is that Olivia and Sebastian go and get married.

The Scenes Alternate Between *Serious* and *Funny*

1) Even though the whole play is a <u>comedy</u>, some scenes are more <u>serious</u> than others.

2) The <u>romantic</u> scenes with Viola, Olivia and Orsino are <u>witty</u> rather than full on belly-laughs.

3) The scenes with Sir Toby and Sir Andrew feature <u>slapstick humour</u> worthy of Jim Carrey.

4) Shakespeare uses the silly <u>subplot</u> about the trick played on Malvolio to break up the stodgy <u>love scenes</u> — otherwise you'd get really sick of people moaning on about how <u>in love</u> they are.

Here's an example from Act 2:

PRETTY SERIOUS

Act 2, Scene 2 — Viola/Cesario loves Orsino and realises that Olivia loves her. It's an odd situation and she's seriously worried about it.

BELLY LAUGHS

Act 2, Scene 3 — Hooray! Sir Andrew and Sir Toby are getting leathered, which is a pretty good laugh. Maria explains the funny trick she wants to play on stuffy Malvolio.

PRETTY SERIOUS

Act 2, Scene 4 — Zzzzz. Orsino and Viola/Cesario are getting all gloopy talking about love. Even Feste's sick of Orsino banging on.

BELLY LAUGHS

Act 2, Scene 5 — Phew. Now it's time to play the trick on Malvolio. More frolics from Sir Andrew and Sir Toby.

> The funny/serious/funny/serious pattern goes on through most of the play.

This darn play, I don't know whether to laugh or cry...

If you didn't spot the 'Prisoner' gag at the top of the page, then go and revise your late 60's psychedelic TV shows. You don't want to be caught out if the essay question is 'Who is Number 1?'

How Shakespeare Makes Things Funny

He does, kind of...

There are Lots of Comic Misunderstandings

People aren't always what they seem in *Twelfth Night*. Viola/Cesario and Sebastian look <u>absolutely identical</u>. This leads to a whole heap of <u>comic misunderstandings</u>.

Orsino <u>doesn't realise</u> Viola is a <u>girl</u> — who really likes him.

> (Aside) Yet, a barful strife!
> Whoe'er I woo, myself would be his wife.
> Act 1, Scene 4, 40-41

<u>Sebastian</u> doesn't know why Olivia has <u>thrown herself</u> at him — but he's still pretty chuffed.

> What relish is in this?...
> If it be thus to dream, still let me sleep
> Act 4, Scene 1, 54-57

<u>Maria's trick</u> on Malvolio leads to even <u>more misunderstanding</u>. Olivia doesn't realise that Malvolio is trying to seduce her and thinks he's <u>gone mad</u>.

> Why, this is very midsummer madness.
> Act 4, Scene 1, 54-57

Some of the Jokes are Visual

Sir Andrew <u>dances</u>, in Act 1, Scene 3.

Malvolio arrives <u>sober</u> and <u>angry</u> at the <u>party</u> in Act 2, Scene 3.

In Act 3, Scene 4 Malvolio enters wearing <u>yellow stockings</u> and grinning like an idiot.

Sir Andrew and Viola are unwillingly pushed together to <u>fight</u> in Act 3, Scene 4.

There are Funny Lines in the Dialogue

Some of the lines are <u>genuinely witty</u> — Feste gets most of the best ones.

> The lady bade take away the fool;
> therefore I say again, take her away.
> Act 1, Scene 5, 45-46

Some of the characters are given <u>foolish lines</u> to make the audience laugh — especially Sir Andrew.

> I am a great eater of beef, and I believe
> that does harm to my wit.
> Act 1, Scene 3, 84

People Behave Inappropriately

1) People behave <u>outside</u> the usual <u>social norms</u> in *Twelfth Night* — Viola <u>dresses up</u> as a <u>boy</u> and does stuff girls wouldn't usually have got up to in the <u>early seventeenth century</u>.

2) Some of Shakespeare's jokes are a bit <u>snobby</u> — he writes about a <u>servant</u> thinking he has a chance of getting together with his <u>boss</u> as if it was completely <u>inappropriate</u> and laughable.

3) There's a big difference between the <u>romantic, richer</u> characters and the <u>poorer, more down-to-earth</u> characters in the play. This <u>contrast</u> is sometimes used to get the laughs — for example when <u>Sir Toby</u> is <u>very drunk</u> in front of Olivia in Act 1, Scene 5.

Hee hee... ha, hA, ha! OO hoo HOO (grunt) .... err ... I don't get it...

It's OK, don't worry if you don't find the play <u>side-splitting</u> — just make sure you know why it <u>should</u> be. Then you can laugh in the right places and pretend it's funny like everyone else does... the truth is no one finds it funny. Because it's not. It's rubbish.

How Shakespeare Keeps You Interested

Shakespeare was pretty good at second-guessing the <u>reactions</u> of the audience. You need to be able to spot the bits where he <u>manipulates</u> the audience.

Shakespeare <u>Prepares</u> You For What Will <u>Happen</u>

Shakespeare sometimes gives <u>clues</u> about what's going to happen.

1) <u>Viola</u> harps on about missing her brother who might be drowned. That means that you know who <u>Sebastian</u> is when he turns up on shore in Act 2.

> My brother, he is in Elysium.
> Perchance he is not drowned:
> Act 1, Scene 2, 4-5

> ...it was said she
> much resembled me,
> Act 2, Scene 1, 21-22

2) Sebastian and Viola are <u>identical</u>, so you can guess that there'll be all sorts of crazy misunderstandings when people <u>mix them up</u>.

3) <u>Antonio</u> says he shouldn't go to Orsino's court in case he's <u>arrested</u>, but then goes anyway — so it's no surprise when he gets into <u>trouble</u> the minute he arrives.

> I have many enemies in Orsino's court,
> Act 2, Scene 1, 39

4) It seems odd for Antonio to lend Sebastian his <u>purse</u> in Act 3, Scene 3 — but it turns out to be important when Antonio asks <u>Viola/Cesario</u> for his purse back later.

> What will you do, now my necessity
> Makes me to ask you for my purse?
> Act 3, Scene 4, 302-303

5) Viola keeps dropping <u>hints</u> that she <u>loves Orsino</u>. When they talk about ideal women, she describes someone like <u>Orsino</u> — so it doesn't seem so mad when they get together after she reveals she's a <u>girl</u>.

> ORSINO   What kind of woman
>   is't?
> VIOLA   Of your complexion.
>   Act 2, Scene 4, 24

Some <u>Questions</u> Are Left Open for Ages

Shakespeare doesn't like to give all the <u>answers</u> at once. He often strings the audience along.

1) Viola works out that Olivia <u>fancies</u> her in Act 2, Scene 2 — but she decides not to do anything about it. You just know it's going to lead to <u>trouble</u>, but you have to wait until Act 3 to see what Olivia does next.

> ...what means this lady?
> Fortune forbid my outside have not charmed her!
> Act 2, Scene 2, 14-15

2) There's a big <u>build-up</u> to the fight between Sir Andrew and Viola/Cesario, and you can't tell who'll win if they fight. In the end Antonio <u>breaks up</u> the fight.

Shakespeare <u>dots around</u> between storylines, so you have to wait to see what happens to a character (see page 36).

> Good fool, some ink, paper and light, and
> convey what I will set down to my lady.
> Act 4, Scene 2, 102-103

3) When Malvolio's locked in the dark room he asks Feste for <u>writing materials</u>. You're not shown him writing the letter, but in Act 5 the letter he wrote proves that he's <u>not mad</u>.

4) The <u>love triangle</u> between Viola, Olivia and Orsino goes on for most of the play, and only gets sorted out <u>really quickly</u> at the end of Act 5.

Sorry, I nodded off for a moment there...

...What? Is it morning already? Where am I? Oh yes, as I was saying, Shakespeare really does know how to keep you <u>interested</u>. My sleepiness is nothing to do with him, honestly. Zzzzzzzzzz.

How the Atmosphere is Created

Twelfth Night is a romantic comedy — Shakespeare used every trick he knew to make it <u>fun</u>. He wanted the play to <u>be a good laugh</u>, so he tried to keep the atmosphere <u>light</u>.

The Settings are Exotic and Pleasant

Shakespeare didn't just throw a dart at a map. He chose the <u>settings</u> in the play for a <u>reason</u>.

1) The play's set in Illyria, which would have sounded pretty <u>exotic</u> to most people from England (see page 12).

2) Loads of the play takes place outside in <u>Olivia's garden</u> in the <u>daytime</u>, which lets the audience know that everything in the play is happy and fun.

3) The rest of the play is set in Orsino's grand <u>palace</u> or in Olivia's nice <u>posh house</u>. The only <u>dingy</u> setting is the dark room that Malvolio gets locked in.

Language and Music are Used to Create Atmosphere

In Shakespeare's day they <u>didn't</u> use any scenery, so he had to create atmosphere in other ways.

1) There's loads of <u>music</u> in *Twelfth Night*. Feste sings lots of <u>songs</u>, Sir Andrew does a crazy dance in Act 1 and there are tons of references to music too. It helps to make the atmosphere <u>lively</u>, <u>fun</u> and <u>romantic</u> — you know from the start that the play's <u>not</u> going to involve misery or death.

Even the first line in the play is about music.

> If music be the food of love, play on —
> Act 1, Scene 1, 1

2) Different types of <u>dances</u> get mentions too, especially when the <u>sillier</u> characters like Sir Andrew and Sir Toby are around. It shows that they're all just <u>messing around</u> and <u>having fun</u>.

> Why dost thou not go to church in a galliard and come home in a coranto? My very walk should be a jig — I would not so much as make water but in a sink-a-pace.
> Act 1, Scene 3, 111-114

3) The mood gets more <u>serious</u> and <u>romantic</u> when characters talk about <u>love</u>. The characters use <u>formal</u> (and quite poncy) language, unlike funnier characters such as Sir Toby.

Orsino thinks he's the <u>best lover</u> in the world, and he speaks very seriously about his <u>devotion</u> to Olivia.

> For such as I am, all true lovers are,
> Unstaid and skittish in all motions else,
> Save in the constant image of the creature
> That is beloved.
> Act 2, Scene 4, 15-18

Viola thinks that it's OK for people to <u>suffer</u> for love. The language she uses makes the play a lot more <u>sombre</u> (for a while, anyway).

> She never told her love,
> But let concealment, like a worm i' th' bud,
> Feed on her damask cheek:
> Act 2, Scene 4, 107-109

'Twelfth Night' — or 'What You Welkin'...

Examiners just love it when you mention how Shakespeare <u>creates</u> a particular <u>atmosphere</u>. And if you learn the moves to some Shakespearean dances you might pick up extra marks too.

Revision Summary

Shakespeare was in his thirties at the end of the Sixteenth century. I can just imagine him dancing like a clown and making a fool of himself at the New Year's party. Or maybe he stayed at home and wrote a rubbish poem instead. We just don't know. But what we do know is that he wrote complicated plays just to confuse you when you're writing essays. Answer these questions on stagecraft and when you've finished do them again until you know them off by heart.

1) What are the 2 main plot lines in _Twelfth Night_?

2) What's the difference between the names of the characters in the two stories?

3) Give some differences between the use of language in the two stories.

4) Give examples of different attitudes to love in the two stories.

5) What 2 things did Shakespeare have to decide when he was structuring the play?

6) Give an example of romantic scenes building up to the most important scene.

7) Give an example of comic scenes building up to the funniest scene.

8) Why might Shakespeare have put a few boring scenes into the play?

9) Complete the sentence: Scenes that just move the plot forward are normally...
   a) ...long   b) ...short   c) ...purple and they wear 10-gallon hats.

10) Why does Shakespeare put serious scenes next to funny scenes?

11) Give examples of four different types of humour in _Twelfth Night_.

12) Write down 3 examples of characters in the play behaving inappropriately.

13) Give 5 examples showing how Shakespeare prepares the audience for what's about to happen.

14) Write down 4 situations in the play that are left open for ages.

15) A lot of _Twelfth Night_ takes place outside in daylight. How does that affect the mood?

16) Did they use scenery to create atmosphere in Shakespeare's time?

17) Name two things that make _Twelfth Night_ lively and a bit silly.

18) What are the characters usually talking about when the mood gets serious?

There once was a man from Fishguard,
Who had a packet of lard.
He said "I don't like Twelfth Night,
The humour is trite."
And decided to deep-fry the Bard.

What Happens in Act One

This section tells the story of the play — showing what every scene's about.
Go through the play one scene at a time until you understand the whole story.

Scene One — The Duke's Madly in Love

This scene is nice and short. This drippy fellow starts telling us all about love —
straightaway we know what the play's all about.

1 Orsino is in love
Orsino talks about his love. He asks for more music to
help him enjoy it, and then suddenly changes his mind.
He can't concentrate on anything. lines 1-15

2 Curio invites him to go and hunt
Curio is just trying to distract Orsino, but the Duke
turns his words into an image of his love for Olivia.
lines 16-23

3 Valentine comes in with a message from Olivia
Orsino had sent Valentine to tell Olivia about his love,
but Valentine didn't get in to see her. Her maid told
him that Olivia's still mourning the death of her brother.
lines 23-32

4 Orsino imagines Olivia falling in love with him
He compares the love she feels for her brother to the
love she might one day feel for him, and imagines he
will be king of her heart. lines 33-41

Duke Orsino has got it bad.
Everything around him reminds him
of his love — the music, the
invitation to go hunting, even
Olivia's grief for her dead brother.

Scene Two — Viola's been Shipwrecked near Illyria

Sebastian.

Seb's dead, already.

Nah, I doubt it. I reckon
he'll turn up later on.

Viola doesn't worry about the future —
she thinks it'll all work out fine.

What else may hap, to time I will commit.
(60)

She says something similar
at the end of Act 2, Scene 2.

1 Viola, the Captain and his sailors arrive in Illyria
Viola is worried that her brother might have drowned.
The Captain says that he saw Viola's brother hanging on
to a piece of wood floating in the water. lines 1-20

2 The Captain knows the area and all the gossip
It turns out that the Captain was brought up nearby,
and he tells Viola that Duke Orsino rules the area. He
also tells her about Orsino's love for Olivia. Viola says
she understands why Olivia's shut herself away.
lines 21-46

3 Viola decides to disguise herself as a boy
Viola asks the Captain to help her become a servant of
the Duke. She believes that everything will sort itself
out in time. lines 47-64

Viola's like the dishes — she's all washed up...

These scenes are both short and slightly boring. In the first scene all you see is Orsino banging on
about how in love he is. Mind you, both scenes give you quite a bit of information — Olivia's
brother's dead, and Viola's brother might be drowned. It's all useful, so get on and learn it.

What Happens in Act One

It's no good <u>rushing</u> this section. In fact that's a <u>truly terrible</u> idea. You might need to write about <u>any scene</u> in the exam. Recognising <u>where</u> a scene comes in the story will be a <u>huge help</u>.

Scene Three — Sir Toby and Maria Tease Sir Andrew

At last — here's a nice jolly scene to make a <u>change</u> from the last two.

The <u>real reason</u> Sir Toby is friends with Sir Andrew is because he has <u>money</u>:

> Why, he has three thousand ducats a year. (19)

Everything else Sir Toby says about him here is a <u>joke</u>.

Good Mistress Accost, I desire your better aquaintance.

Why are they laughing?

1 Maria tells Sir Toby that Olivia is cross with him
Maria warns Sir Toby about his late nights and drunkenness. She tells him to be careful. Sir Toby refuses and makes a joke of it. lines 1-11

2 Maria and Sir Toby argue about Sir Andrew
Maria warns Sir Toby that Olivia's also angry about him spending so much time with Sir Andrew. Maria says Andrew is a money-waster, an idiot, a drunk and a coward. Sir Toby jokingly praises Andrew's gifts at music and foreign languages. lines 12-38

3 Sir Andrew comes in
Sir Toby and Maria make fun of Sir Andrew. He doesn't understand their jokes. Maria leaves. lines 39-71

4 Sir Andrew and Sir Toby have a chat
Sir Andrew is miserable. He says he plans to go home. Sir Toby changes his mind and convinces him not to give up on Olivia. Sir Andrew decides to stay and they start making lots of jokes. lines 72-123

Scene Four — Viola's Made a Big Hit with Orsino

This is the <u>first time</u> we see Viola dressed as a <u>boy</u>.

1 Viola has become Orsino's favourite
Viola is dressed as a boy and calls herself Cesario. The Duke is already fond of Cesario. lines 1-8

2 The Duke sends Cesario to Olivia on his behalf
Orsino has told Viola/Cesario all his secrets. Now he sends Cesario to Olivia to tell Olivia that he loves her. lines 9-25

3 Orsino thinks Olivia will listen to Cesario
He thinks Olivia will be more likely to listen to a youth. He says that Cesario looks and sounds more like a woman than a man, so Olivia will listen. lines 26-39

4 Viola is in love with the Duke
She'll go and talk to Olivia, but at the end of the scene she tells us she's really in love with the Duke herself. lines 40-41

Blimey — <u>three days</u> have already gone by since Scene 2:

Dude looks like a lady.

> He hath known you but three days, and already you are no stranger. (2-3)

This bit's a <u>joke</u> — Orsino <u>doesn't know</u> that Cesario <u>really is</u> a girl, but the <u>audience</u> <u>does</u>. Shakespeare's having a <u>laugh</u>.

Isn't that a Bond film — Orsino Royale...

<u>Don't</u> get muddled — you need to know the <u>order</u> things happen in and <u>where</u> they're happening.

What Happens in Act One

Here's where the play starts to get really <u>interesting</u> — Olivia <u>meets</u> Viola/Cesario and <u>falls in love</u>.

Scene Five — Viola/Cesario turns up at Olivia's House

First of all you get to see the other two <u>main comedy characters</u> in action — <u>Feste</u> and <u>Malvolio</u>.

1 Feste's in trouble with Olivia
He's been skiving somewhere — and Maria warns him that Olivia's on the warpath. She tells him she won't make any excuses for him — Olivia may well throw him out. lines 1-31

2 He's got to make Olivia laugh — or else
Olivia and Malvolio appear. She asks for Feste to be taken away. He starts cracking jokes to show off his wit. Olivia is quite amused, and tells Malvolio off for being rude to Feste. lines 32-86

3 Maria says there's a young man at the gate
Maria says someone's at the gate. Olivia tells Malvolio to send him away if he comes from the Duke. Olivia warns Feste not to fool too much. lines 87-102

4 Sir Toby arrives home drunk (again)
Olivia asks him who's at the gate. Toby's too drunk to say. lines 103-125

5 Malvolio comes back with news
The young man at the gate's determined to speak to Olivia. She is curious and decides to speak to him, but puts her veil on first. lines 126-150

It looks like Feste's been <u>gone</u> for a while. He <u>has</u> to <u>impress</u> Olivia to get his <u>job</u> back.

Viola/Cesario speaks very <u>sweetly</u> to Olivia. She wants to do her job <u>well</u> to <u>please</u> Orsino.

Olivia's <u>lying</u> — she just wants to give Cesario a <u>present</u> so that he'll <u>visit</u> her again soon.

6 It's not really a man, it's Viola/Cesario
Viola/Cesario comes in and speaks to Olivia. Olivia is enchanted by Cesario, and sends her attendants away. Olivia takes off her veil, and Cesario sees her face. Viola/Cesario tells Olivia how in love the Duke is, but Olivia's only interested in Cesario. lines 153-264

7 Uh oh — Olivia's falling in love
Olivia wants Cesario to come again. She offers him money, but Viola/Cesario refuses and leaves. Olivia's very impressed with Cesario's looks and actions, and realises she's falling in love with him. lines 265-274

8 Olivia sends Malvolio after Cesario
Olivia calls Malvolio and gives him a ring to take to Cesario. She tells Malvolio that Cesario left it, and she wants to return it. Malvolio takes the ring. lines 274-287

Feste and the twins — I hate all this cloning around...

This Viola/Cesario business is confusing. Just remember — everyone <u>thinks</u> she's a boy. Olivia <u>doesn't</u> know she's fallen in love with a <u>woman</u> dressed as a man, but the <u>audience</u> does. It's all a big <u>joke</u>.

What Happens in Act Two

OK, this is where you meet twin number two, Sebastian. Now it starts to get really confusing.

Scene One — Here's Viola's brother, Sebastian

Sebastian's been saved too — that's a good start.

1 Sebastian was rescued by Antonio
Sebastian's been with Antonio a while, but now he wants to move on. Antonio offers to go with him, but Sebastian's still sad. He would rather travel alone.   lines 1-13

2 Sebastian thinks Viola is dead
Sebastian explains that he has a twin sister who was drowned in the shipwreck, and he's really upset. lines 13-36

3 He's heading for Orsino's court
He says goodbye to Antonio. He says he's almost ready to cry, and leaves. Antonio tells the audience he has enemies in Orsino's court, so he shouldn't follow Sebastian, but he will anyway. lines 36-42

My poor sister! Ah, Viola!

See, I told you. Sebastian's alright. He's been rescued by another ship.

You've seen this play before, haven't you?

Scene Two — Things Get More Difficult for Viola

Now it's all starting to become clear to Viola — she's in a real pickle.
She loves Orsino, Orsino loves Olivia, and Olivia loves...her. Oops.

Malvolio speaks to Viola/Cesario coldly and rather rudely.

Duke Orsino loves Olivia.

The duke is attracted to Viola, but thinks she's a man.

Olivia loves Cesario.

Cesario (Viola) loves the duke.

Viola doesn't do anything about the problem. She's going to leave it to sort itself out.

1 Malvolio gives the ring to Cesario
Malvolio catches up with Viola/Cesario and delivers the message from Olivia. He throws the ring down on the ground. lines 1-13

2 Viola's left scratching her head
Viola didn't leave a ring with Olivia. She suspects Olivia has fallen in love with her as a boy, and realises her disguise has worked too well. She says to herself it's easy for a woman to fall in love with the wrong man because women are weak. lines 14-30

3 Only time'll sort out this mess
Orsino loves Olivia but he doesn't stand a chance, Viola loves Orsino but she doesn't stand a chance, and Olivia loves Cesario — and she really doesn't have a chance. It's too tricky for Viola to solve. lines 30-38

Playing Viola — a job for a musician perhaps...

These two scenes are dead important — it's the first time we see Sebastian. Antonio's decision to follow him is crucial for later, so don't forget it. It's also where Viola realises the mess she's in.

What Happens in Act Two

It's <u>party time</u> in this scene. Toby's <u>drunk</u> — in fact he's slaughtered — and so's Sir Andrew. They decide to have a <u>sing-song</u>, but you can bet Malvolio <u>isn't</u> amused.

Scene Three — Malvolio _has a_ barney _with_ Sir Toby

1 Andrew and Toby are chatting drunkenly
Sir Toby makes lots of jokes that Andrew doesn't get. They both demand more wine. lines 1-13

2 Feste comes to join the fun
Sir Andrew and Sir Toby ask him for a song. He jokes with them until they pay him. He sings two love songs, then they all sing together. lines 14-65

3 Maria's had enough of their racket
She warns them to keep the noise down, in case Olivia calls Malvolio to come down and throw them out. They carry on singing. lines 66-79

4 Malvolio tries to break up the party
He storms in and shouts at them. He threatens to have Sir Toby kicked out. lines 80-93

5 The lads carry on singing anyway
Sir Toby tells Malvolio that just because he's a goody-goody, it shouldn't mean that anyone else should be denied their fun. lines 94-112

6 Malvolio storms off in huff
Malvolio says he's telling on Maria to Olivia. Maria's not impressed. lines 113-115

Feste <u>isn't</u> drunk — he's there to <u>make money</u> out of them, and joins the fun for a <u>laugh</u>.

If I do not gull him into a nayword, and make him a common recreation, do not think I have wit enough to lie straight in my bed: I know I can do it. (124-127)

Cunning Plan

Maria <u>can't</u> answer Malvolio back to his face in case she <u>ends up</u> in <u>trouble</u> with Olivia — she has to be more <u>sneaky</u> to get her <u>revenge</u>.

7 Maria's got a plan for revenge
Sir Andrew and Sir Toby want to challenge Malvolio to a duel, but Maria's got an idea for making a complete fool of him. lines 116-127

8 Maria describes Malvolio's faults
He's pompous. He thinks he's the bee's knees, and thinks anyone who looks at him will love him. lines 128-149

9 Here's Maria's cunning plan
She'll write a love letter to Malvolio in Olivia's handwriting. He'll think Olivia's in love with him. It's an ace plan. Maria leaves. lines 150-162

10 Sir Toby and Sir Andrew stay up longer
Sir Toby talks about how great Maria is, and tells Andrew to send for more money. They decide to stay up and have another drink. lines 163-176

A family of Scottish jokers — a punning clan...

Right — this is where the <u>seeds</u> of the trick are sown. Everyone is <u>seriously narked</u> with Malvolio by the end of this scene. He's <u>spoiled</u> the party and <u>threatened</u> to <u>tell Olivia</u> — now it's <u>revenge time</u>.

ACT 2 SCENE 4

What Happens in Act Two

The <u>tension</u> between <u>Viola/Cesario</u> and <u>Orsino</u> is building up now. Viola is <u>in love</u> with Orsino, and it's starting to <u>show</u>. If only he knew Cesario was really a woman...

Scene Four — Orsino and Cesario Talk about Love

Orsino <u>doesn't</u> mention <u>Olivia</u> until later in the scene — he's just <u>enjoying</u> being in love.

> Go on, then, who do you fancy? You can tell me...

> You'd get the wrong idea.

1 Orsino asks to hear a song
Curio says that Feste sang the song, and he's not here. Orsino sends Curio off to look for him. lines 1-12

2 Orsino tells Cesario about love
He tells Viola/Cesario to remember him and his odd behaviour if he ever falls in love. lines 13-18

3 He asks for Viola/Cesario's opinion
Orsino thinks Viola/Cesario knows about love. He asks who Viola/Cesario is in love with. lines 19-23

4 It sounds surprisingly familiar...
Viola/Cesario describes the woman as being like the Duke. Orsino thinks she must be too old. lines 23-39

This bit can be really <u>funny</u>. Viola's talking about <u>Orsino</u>, but he <u>doesn't</u> realise it. The audience <u>does</u> — which makes it <u>comical</u>.

The song <u>breaks up</u> the tension between Orsino and Cesario.

5 In comes Feste to sing his song
Feste sings that being in love is like dying, and gets paid. He thinks Orsino's being self-indulgent. lines 40-75

6 Orsino sends Feste and Curio away
Orsino tells Viola/Cesario to go to Olivia again. Viola/Cesario tries to explain that Olivia doesn't love Orsino. He doesn't believe it. lines 76-89

7 They talk about love
Orsino says that men's love is stronger than women's love. Viola/Cesario tells Orsino that women can feel just as strongly as men. She gives the example of a sister — but she's really talking about her own feelings for Orsino. lines 90-121

> You idiot! This is Twelfth Night. We're in the wrong play!

> "I am slain by a fair cruel maid: My shroud of white, stuck all with dew, O prepare it."

> Blimey. I'll have to remember this one.

ORSINO   But died thy sister of her love, my boy?
VIOLA   I am all the daughters of my fathers house,
          And all the brothers too: and yet I know not.
                                                    (116-118)

The state of British tennis — let's talk about love...

Viola <u>can't hide</u> the fact that she's in love with Orsino, try as she might. It's a good job he's so wrapped up in <u>himself</u>. Remember — he <u>doesn't know</u> she's really a <u>girl</u>, he thinks she's a <u>boy</u>.

What Happens in Act Two

This scene's one of the <u>funniest</u> in the play. It looks really funny on stage — the <u>audience</u> can <u>see</u> the characters hiding behind the hedge and can <u>hear</u> them discussing what Malvolio's doing.

Scene Five — Time to Play the <u>Trick</u> on <u>Malvolio</u>

You've had a taster in scenes 2 and 3, but here's where Malvolio <u>shows</u> exactly how <u>pompous</u> and <u>arrogant</u> he is — until the <u>trick</u> makes him look <u>ridiculous</u>.

1 Toby, Andrew and Fabian are ready for the fun
Fabian's another servant with an old score to settle against Malvolio. lines 1-11

2 They hide in the hedge
Malvolio's coming. Maria tells them to hide in the hedge and drops the letter in the path. lines 12-19

3 Malvolio already thinks Olivia fancies him
He thinks she finds him good-looking. lines 20-24

4 This gets the others quite worked up
They call him a rogue. Sir Andrew wants to beat him up. lines 25-36

5 Malvolio fantasises about marrying Olivia
He'd boss more people around. He'd tell Sir Toby off for drinking and stop him seeing Sir Andrew. lines 37-72

Malvolio's got him into <u>trouble</u> with Olivia in the past.

Why are we hiding behind a giant hedgehog, Sir Toby?

They couldn't find a hedge.

Ask a stupid question.

Sir Toby and Fabian keep shushing each other in case Malvolio <u>hears</u> them.

By this point, Sir Toby's ready to <u>throttle</u> him — Fabian has to <u>hold him back</u>.

Maria wrote some of the <u>letters</u> of <u>Malvolio's name</u> in the poem, so the <u>clues</u> are pretty <u>hard</u> to miss.

Oh, I love it when you smile at me that way. And oh, you look so handsome in those stockings.

6 Now he sees the letter
He recognises Olivia's handwriting and the seal on the letter. He decides to read it. lines 73-84

7 The trick's working
There's a love poem in the letter, and Malvolio picks up clues that it's about him. The others watch him from the hedge and make comments. lines 85-130

8 The letter tells Malvolio to do stupid things
He should be even more pompous. He should be rude to Sir Toby and the servants to prove he loves Olivia. He should wear yellow stockings. lines 130-140

9 Malvolio falls for it hook, line and sinker
He's very excited by the letter. He imagines that Olivia really will like his yellow stockings. The letter asks him to smile all the time. lines 141-157

10 Toby and Fabian think it's hilarious
Fabian says he wouldn't give this up for a thousand pounds. Toby says he could marry Maria for this. Maria tells them to watch how Malvolio acts in front of Olivia — she's going to hate it. lines 158-183

Malvolio is a gull — I thought that was Albert Ross...

Watch out — this is one of those scenes where you need to know exactly <u>what</u> happens <u>when</u>. It's <u>really important</u> to remember that Malvolio <u>thinks</u> Olivia fancies him <u>before</u> he reads the letter.

ACT 3 SCENES 1-2

What Happens in Act Three

Oh dear — this act's all a bit <u>lovey-dovey</u> to start with, but you've <u>still</u> got to <u>know</u> it all.

Scene One — *Olivia* admits She *Loves* Viola/Cesario

1 Viola/Cesario's joking with Feste
Feste makes a lot of clever jokes and comments. Viola/Cesario joins in. Feste leaves. Viola/Cesario is impressed with his wit. lines 1-62

2 Sir Toby and Sir Andrew appear
They're trying to put Viola/Cesario off. Andrew's worried that Olivia likes Cesario. lines 63-84

3 Olivia wants to see Viola/Cesario alone
She sends Maria and the others away. Viola/Cesario wants to talk about Orsino's love for Olivia, but Olivia has other ideas. lines 85-103

4 Olivia tells Viola/Cesario she fancies him
Viola/Cesario isn't interested, but Olivia keeps on flirting. lines 104-131

5 Olivia asks what Cesario thinks of her
Viola/Cesario says Olivia doesn't know what she's doing, then admits that she's pretending to be something she isn't. lines 132-137

6 Olivia loves Viola/Cesario even more
She's still smitten, but Viola/Cesario says no woman will be her love. lines 138-157

She understands that Feste must be pretty <u>clever</u> to be able to play the fool so well.

Viola/Cesario <u>tries</u> to put Olivia off, but it only makes things <u>worse</u>:

> O, what a deal of scorn looks beautiful
> In the contempt and anger of his lip.
> (138-139)

= Ooh, he's beautiful when he's angry...

Scene Two — *Sir Andrew's Jealous of Cesario*

Maria's <u>dead pleased</u> that her plan worked.

1 Sir Andrew's seen Olivia and Cesario together
He's upset. Fabian argues that Olivia did it deliberately to make Sir Andrew jealous. lines 1-28

2 Sir Toby suggests a duel
He says Olivia will be impressed if Sir Andrew fights Viola/Cesario. Sir Andrew goes off to write a challenge. lines 29-46

3 Fabian and Sir Toby laugh at Sir Andrew
Sir Toby tells Fabian he's been living off Andrew's money. They think the idea of Sir Andrew fighting a duel with Cesario is very funny. lines 47-58

4 Maria's got news about Malvolio
Malvolio's going about with yellow stockings and a constant grin. Maria says it makes him even more annoying. They all go to watch him. lines 59-74

Andrew's jealous of Cesario — he understands girls so well...

Tricky times for <u>Viola</u> — don't forget this is the <u>first time</u> Olivia's <u>said clearly</u> she <u>loves</u> Cesario.

What Happens in Act Three

It keeps getting <u>more complicated</u>. Now <u>Sebastian</u>'s in town <u>as well as</u> Viola.

Scene Three — Antonio lends Sebastian his Purse

Careful — this scene's <u>dead important</u> for things that happen <u>later</u> in the play.

1 Antonio's caught up with Sebastian
Antonio's followed Sebastian to make sure he's alright. lines 1-18

2 Sebastian suggests they go sightseeing
Antonio refuses — he fought a sea battle against Orsino's ships once. He's afraid he'll be recognised and arrested. lines 18-38

3 Antonio gives Sebastian his purse
He wants Sebastian to buy himself something nice. They arrange to meet at the inn in an hour. Sebastian goes off. lines 38-49

Scene Four — Malvolio Makes a Fool of Himself

Yep — it's the bit you've been waiting for... Malvolio makes a <u>prat</u> of himself.

Malvolio's <u>convinced</u> he's doing the right thing.

Cheer up, mate. She's just playing hard to get.

Making a fool of him is <u>one</u> thing, but <u>locking him up</u> as if he <u>really is</u> mad is pretty cruel.

1 Olivia's waiting for Cesario
She's sad so she sends for Malvolio. Maria says he's acting oddly. lines 1-15

2 Malvolio comes in smiling
Olivia is confused. Malvolio tries to be charming and sexy. lines 16-35

3 Malvolio brings up the letter
He mentions various lines from the letter. Olivia is even more confused. lines 36-55

4 Olivia doesn't know what he's on about
She thinks he's gone mad. She goes to meet Cesario, and leaves Toby to take charge of Malvolio. lines 56-59

5 Malvolio thinks it's all going his way
He's sure it's going to plan. lines 60-77

6 Sir Toby, Fabian and Maria laugh at him
They talk to Malvolio as if he's mad. He's rude to them — like the letter told him to be. lines 78-114

7 They decide to lock him up
They want to keep the joke going for a bit longer. lines 117-128

Love — Malvolio's mad for it...

Watch out — this is a really <u>long</u> act, and it's <u>complicated</u> too. You've still got to <u>know</u> it well though. Turn the page over and <u>scribble down</u> a quick <u>summary</u> of the act so far — then <u>learn</u> it.

ACT 3 SCENE 4 — What Happens in Act Three

This scene's a <u>whopper</u> — it goes on and on.
You've got to know <u>what happens</u> and <u>when</u> it does, or you could end up in a right <u>muddle</u>.

More Scene Four — Building up to a Fight

Don't fret, just <u>work through</u> the scene <u>bit by bit</u> and you'll get there.

8 Sir Andrew's written his challenge
Sir Toby reads it out and it's dreadful. Sir Toby sends Andrew off the wrong way. Toby won't give Viola/Cesario the letter — it's too badly written to scare anyone. He decides to challenge Cesario by word of mouth instead. lines 129-177

9 Olivia's still trying to charm Viola/Cesario
Olivia gives a picture of herself. Viola/Cesario says it'd be better if she gave her love to Orsino. Olivia leaves. lines 178-194

10 Sir Toby appears, and tries to scare Viola/Cesario
Sir Toby makes Sir Andrew out to be very brave and fierce. lines 195-226

11 Viola/Cesario tries to make excuses
Viola/Cesario really doesn't want to fight, but Toby says there's no way out. Toby leaves but Fabian keeps winding Viola/Cesario up, saying Andrew is a skilled fighter. lines 226-245

Viola/Cesario <u>wouldn't</u> have any <u>training</u> in swordfighting because she was a <u>girl</u> — the idea of a <u>duel</u> would be really <u>scary</u> for her.

<u>Here's</u> where the business about the <u>purse</u> comes in. Antonio thinks that <u>Viola/Cesario</u> is <u>Sebastian</u>, so he <u>asks her</u> for his purse back before he gets carted off to prison.

12 Meanwhile Toby tells Andrew to be afraid
He tells him Cesario is a great fighter. Sir Andrew has second thoughts. lines 246-258

13 They get ready to fight — unwillingly
Viola's almost ready to admit she's a girl. Andrew doesn't want to fight either. lines 259-279

14 Antonio to the rescue!
He mistakes Viola/Cesario for Sebastian. He comes rushing in and threatens Sir Andrew. lines 280-286

15 The police turn up to arrest Antonio
They recognise him from the old battle he fought against Orsino. They arrest him. lines 287-300

16 Antonio asks for his money
He asks for his purse, thinking it's Sebastian, but Viola/Cesario doesn't understand. She offers him some of her own money. Antonio thinks he's been betrayed and curses Sebastian. He is taken away. lines 300-342

17 Hurrah — Viola realises Sebastian must be alive
She realises Antonio thought she was Sebastian, which means her brother might be alive somewhere. lines 343-354

18 Sir Toby thinks Viola/Cesario's a coward
Even Andrew thinks he can beat him now. lines 355-364

A diamond of a fight — a real jewel...

Phew, that was a stonker of a scene to finish off Act Three. Get the <u>order</u> of events in <u>scene 4</u> good and clear — <u>first</u> the <u>Malvolio</u> stuff, then <u>Toby</u> and the gang, then the <u>challenge</u> and the <u>duel</u>.

What Happens in Act Four

Phew — you'd think things had got about as <u>muddled</u> as they could get... but you'd be wrong.

Scene One — Sebastian gets Mistaken for Cesario

1 **Feste mistakes Sebastian for Cesario**
   Feste's been sent to get Viola/Cesario. Sebastian doesn't know him and refuses. He gives Feste money. lines 1-20

2 **Sir Andrew attacks Sebastian**
   He hits Sebastian, thinking he's Cesario, but Sebastian hits him back, and draws his dagger. lines 21-23

3 **Sir Toby butts in**
   Toby grabs Sebastian's arm, and Feste goes to get Olivia. Sebastian frees himself, and he and Sir Toby draw their swords. lines 24-38

4 **Olivia arrives just in time**
   She's angry with Toby for fighting Cesario, and sends him away. lines 39-44

5 **She invites Sebastian into the house**
   He's confused, but goes anyway. lines 45-59

It's the <u>second time</u> there's <u>nearly</u> been a swordfight in the play — and <u>both</u> times it was <u>interrupted</u> at the last second. A <u>real</u> swordfight's <u>too serious</u> for a <u>comedy</u>.

Scene Two — Another Trick on Malvolio

It's all got a bit <u>nasty</u> now — Malvolio's really <u>suffering</u>.

1 **Maria gets Feste to dress up as a priest**
   Feste speaks to Malvolio while Toby watches. He tells Malvolio he's mad even though he says he isn't. lines 1-58

2 **Sir Toby sends Feste as himself**
   Malvolio asks Feste for pen and paper and a candle. He carries on insisting he isn't mad. lines 59-123

Scene Three — Olivia Marries Sebastian in a hurry

1 **Sebastian's having a think**
   He's very confused. Nothing is what it seems to be. He couldn't find Antonio, and now a strange lady has taken a fancy to him. lines 1-21

2 **Olivia comes in with a priest**
   She wants to marry Sebastian. lines 22-31

3 **Sebastian agrees straight away.**
   Off they go into the chapel. lines 32-35

Marriage blues — not until after you're wed...

A lot happens <u>quickly</u> in Act Four — the main thing is Olivia <u>marries Sebastian</u>, thinking he's <u>Cesario</u>.

ACT 5 SCENE 1 — What Happens in Act Five

There's <u>only</u> one scene in this act, but it's a <u>biggie</u>. I've broken it into <u>chunks</u> to make it <u>easier</u> to work through. It's the <u>last bit</u> of the play, where things get <u>sorted out</u>.

Scene One — At Last Orsino Goes to See Olivia

1 Fabian's pestering Feste

Feste's got the letter Malvolio wrote, and Fabian's worried — he wants to see it but Feste won't let him look. lines 1-6

2 Orsino arrives to see Olivia

Orsino's finally decided to see Olivia himself. He turns up with Viola/Cesario. He recognises Feste who jokes with him and gets paid for his efforts. Orsino asks Feste to let Olivia know he's there to see her. lines 7-43

3 Antonio is brought in as a prisoner

Orsino recognises him and says he knows him as a notorious pirate. The officers explain how he was arrested. Viola/Cesario tells the Duke that Antonio saved him earlier, but said some strange things as well. Orsino questions Antonio. lines 44-65

4 Antonio tells his story bitterly

He tells how he rescued Sebastian from the wreck and followed him to Illyria out of love. He thinks he saved Sebastian from Toby and Andrew, but Sebastian refused to give him his own money back. Everyone else is confused when Antonio says he's been with Sebastian for three months — Viola/Cesario has been with the Duke all that time. lines 65-89

> The trick on Malvolio's gone a bit <u>too far</u>. Fabian's <u>worried</u> that he'll get into <u>trouble</u> for being part of it.

Need a hand, mate?

That'd be rather nice, thanks.

But Olivia thinks She's Married Cesario

How could you betray me like this?

You've betrayed me. Get lost, I hate you!

> It's <u>confusing enough</u> for everyone else, but it's <u>horrible</u> for <u>Viola</u>. Everyone's suddenly <u>accusing her</u> of all sorts of things she <u>didn't do</u>.

5 Olivia appears — things get really complicated

Olivia arrives and ignores Orsino — she wants to know where Cesario's been. Viola/Cesario tries to make her listen to Orsino, but she won't. Orsino moans about her cruelty and decides that Olivia's in love with someone else. He plots revenge on her. He starts to leave and Viola/Cesario follows. lines 90-126

6 Now Olivia gets confused

She asks where Viola/Cesario is going. Viola/Cesario says she's going with Orsino, whom she loves more than anyone else. Olivia sobs she's been betrayed. She asks why her husband is acting this way. lines 127-136

7 Whoops — Orsino goes mental

Orsino is livid. He thinks Viola/Cesario has betrayed him. Olivia has called the priest to remind Cesario of the marriage. Orsino curses Viola/Cesario and says he never wants to see her/him again. Olivia tells Viola/Cesario not to worry. lines 137-164

What Happens in Act Five

Just when you thought it couldn't get any worse for Viola/Cesario, in comes Sir Andrew...

Sir Andrew and Sir Toby have been Beaten Up

We don't know what's happened to them yet —
the audience is as much in the dark as all the other characters.

Well, here's another fine mess you've got us into.

8 Sir Andrew bursts onto the stage
Sir Andrew comes in covered in blood and calling for a surgeon.
He tells everyone that he and Toby have been injured by Cesario.
Viola/Cesario protests that she's innocent. lines 165-179

9 Sir Toby comes in, helped by Feste
Toby's sober for the first time in the whole play. He's hurt and
trying to find a surgeon. Feste tells him the surgeon's drunk and
Toby is furious. Sir Andrew offers to help, but Toby turns on him
and insults him. They leave the stage. lines 180-197

Sebastian Comes Face to Face with Viola/Cesario

This scene's really emotional — neither Viola nor Sebastian can quite believe that the other one is still alive.

It's a ghost!

It's a very strange mirror.

Hmm — it's convenient that Orsino suddenly falls for Viola, but you've just got to swallow your disbelief, I'm afraid.

10 In comes Sebastian — the penny drops
He apologises to Olivia — it was him who beat up Toby and Andrew.
Everyone else looks at him in astonishment. Orsino says he's amazed how
alike Sebastian and Cesario are. lines 198-206

11 Sebastian spots Antonio straightaway
He's really happy to see his friend. Antonio asks how Sebastian managed
to divide himself in two. Sebastian suddenly sees Viola/Cesario — he's
confused too. He says he never had a brother, but did have a sister. He
asks Viola/Cesario where she comes from. lines 207-220

12 Viola's as shocked as Sebastian
She tells Sebastian she's from Messaline, and that her father and brother
were called Sebastian, but she's so shocked she asks if Sebastian is a ghost.
He tells her he's real, and if she was a woman, he'd know that she was
Viola. lines 221-230

13 They realise who the other one is
They swap family details and Viola says she can bring them to the captain
who has her female clothes. The whole story is clear to everyone.
Sebastian tells Olivia that she nearly married a woman, but luckily she
married him. lines 231-252

14 Orsino realises he loves Viola
He tells Olivia not to worry about her mistake, and says that he will have a
share in the happiness. He asks Viola about all the times she said she loved
him. She promises to swear them over again. Orsino asks to see Viola in
her own clothes, but the Captain who had them is in prison because of a
legal quarrel with Malvolio. lines 253-266

Viola and Sebastian — spot the difference...

The very end of the play builds up loads of tension. Everybody's blaming Viola/Cesario for things she
didn't do. It's tense because you think she's going to get into real trouble — until Sebastian arrives.

ACT 5 SCENE 1 (CONT.)

What Happens in Act Five

Wow — this scene's <u>neverending</u>. Unfortunately, there's a bit <u>more</u> of the story that needs to be <u>sorted out</u> — Malvolio's still <u>locked up</u> in the loony bin.

Everyone's Forgotten about Malvolio

We're really in for it, now.

Does he sound mad to you?

Sounds like an awfully nice fella to me.

15 Olivia decides to send for Malvolio
She wants him to release the Captain, but then she remembers that he's been acting madly. She asks Feste how Malvolio is, and Feste offers her Malvolio's letter. She asks him to read it, but Feste keeps making a joke of it, so she tells Fabian to read it instead. lines 267-287

16 The letter doesn't sound mad at all
Malvolio's letter is very clear and calm. He says he's been wronged and that he has the letter that made him act so strangely. Orsino comments that it doesn't sound very mad. Olivia tells Fabian to fetch Malvolio. lines 288-300

17 Olivia offers to hold Orsino's wedding at her house
Orsino agrees, and asks Viola to marry him. Olivia gets excited that Viola will be her sister. lines 301-11

Malvolio Arrives and He's Absolutely Furious

18 Malvolio isn't a happy bunny
He tells Olivia she has wronged him, but she denies it. He shows her the letter and demands to know why he's been treated so badly. Olivia tells him it isn't her writing, it's Maria's. She realises there's been a trick and offers to let Malvolio judge the case. lines 312-339

19 Fabian comes clean about the trick
Fabian tells Olivia that he and Toby set up the trick, and made Maria write the letter. He says that Toby has married Maria for doing it. Fabian tries to say it was a joke rather than anything serious. Olivia sympathises with Malvolio. lines 340-354

20 Feste stirs things up
He reminds Malvolio about some of the things in the letter. He tells Malvolio he was Sir Topas and that he did it as revenge for Malvolio's rudeness about his fooling (see Act 1 Scene 5). lines 355-361

21 Malvolio storms out swearing revenge
He's still furious, and says he'll be revenged on everybody. line 362

22 Orsino sends someone after him
He wants someone to ask Malvolio to make peace. Then he talks about the wedding, and his love for Viola. lines 363-72

23 Feste sings a final song
It's quite sad, about how fooling starts off innocent and ends up lonely. The play's over and he hopes everyone enjoyed it. lines 373-392

Uh oh. I think Malvolio is a bit miffed.

This bit's very <u>weird</u>. <u>Everyone else</u> seems to be happy, but Malvolio's threatening <u>revenge</u>.

It feels like the play <u>isn't</u> properly <u>finished</u>.

Revenge and sad songs — a laugh a minute...

This last scene really <u>isn't</u> funny. The <u>Malvolio story</u> ends up <u>nastily</u>, and <u>Feste's song</u> is very <u>sad</u>.

Revision Summary

Blimey — I never knew <u>Twelfth Night</u> was so long. That's why it's important to get this section sorted. You don't want to get the events of the play in the wrong order when you write your essay — the examiners will think you don't know what you're on about. Try these revision questions. See if you can work through all of them without looking back over the section.

1) What do we find out about Orsino in Act 1 Scene 1?

2) What do we find out about Olivia in Act 1 Scene 1?

3) Who gets washed up on shore on Act 1 Scene 2?

4) What does Maria say about Sir Andrew in Act 1 Scene 2?

5) In which scene do we see Viola dressed as a boy for the first time?

6) Why is Feste in trouble at the start of Act 1 Scene 5?

7) In which act and scene does Viola meet Olivia?

8) In which act and scene do we find out that Viola's brother survived the shipwreck?

9) Why is Viola in a pickle in Act 2 Scene 2?

10) Who breaks up the party in Act 2 Scene 3?

11) What's Maria's cunning plan?

12) Why is the conversation between Orsino and Viola/Cesario in Act 2 Scene 4 funny?

13) Which characters are watching Malvolio read the letter in Act 2 Scene 5?

14) How does Malvolio react when he reads the letter?

15) In which act and scene does Olivia admit she's in love with Viola/Cesario?

16) How does Sir Andrew react when he sees them together?

17) What does Antonio lend to Sebastian in Act 3 Scene 3?

18) In which act and scene does Malvolio make a complete idiot of himself?

19) What happens to Malvolio as a result?

20) Who sets up the fight between Cesario and Sir Andrew?

21) Who comes and stops the fight?

22) Why is Viola so confused when Antonio asks for money?

23) Who does Sir Andrew end up fighting in Act 4 Scene 1?

24) What happens to Sebastian in Act 4 Scene 3?

25) In which act and scene does Orsino finally go to see Olivia?

26) At what point does everyone work out what's been going on?

Index

Index

And Don't Forget to Write a Cracking Essay

I know you've written a zillion essays before. But read this page anyway.

Write Down a Plan of Your Essay Before You Start

Planning is important because it gets a lot of the tricky thinking out of the way.

> Before you start writing your essay you should:
> 1) Decide how you're going to answer the question.
> 2) Jot down a plan of the points you want to make.
> 3) Make sure you've got enough points for the whole essay.
> 4) Organise the points so they flow on from each other.

You should spend about five minutes planning your essay in an exam.
Don't bother writing the plan in proper sentences — it'd waste time.

It's important to plan coursework essays too — you've got more time so the marker will expect your essay to be well thought out.

Structure Your Essay

Your essay should be structured like this:

INTRODUCTION

1) Give a brief answer to the question you're writing about.

Make it clear how you are going to tackle the topic. Don't agonise over wording — just write something like, "This essay is going to argue that..."

2) Explain your answer in detail and give evidence to back it up.

Write a paragraph for each point you make. Start the paragraph by making the point, then back it up with evidence — examples from *Twelfth Night*.

When you quote lines from the play, use inverted commas and give the act, scene and line numbers.

MIDDLE SECTION — paragraphs expanding your argument

> Although Feste works as a fool, he is one of the most intelligent characters in the play. He tells Olivia, "I wear not motley in my brain" (Act 1, Scene 5, lines 49-50), meaning that his foolishness is only on the outside.

Short quotes are nearly always better than long quotes.

3) Always write a conclusion — a paragraph at the end of your essay that should:

> 1) sum up the most important facts and ideas in your essay.
> 2) give your opinion about the topic.
> 3) argue the same thing as the rest of your essay — don't change your opinion at the last minute.

CONCLUSION

Check Everything at the End

You've got to check your essay for mistakes — in an exam, save a good five minutes for this.

1) Check that your essay includes: an introduction and conclusion that agree with each other, all the points from your original plan, and evidence to back them up.

2) If you want to get rid of something just cross it out. Don't scribble over it.

3) If you've left stuff out write it in a separate section at the end of the essay. Put a star (*) next to both the extra writing and the place you want it to go.

Don't forget to check your spelling and punctuation.

I've got a right to sing the blues...

I've got a right to moan and cry...   my beautiful book is finished...   sob.